Quick Little Devotions

To Make a Big Difference In Your Day

Inspired by Faith

Quick Little Devotions
©Product Concept Mfg., Inc.

Quick Little Devotions
ISBN 978-0-9886719-6-6

Published by Product Concept Mfg., Inc.
2175 N. Academy Circle #200, Colorado Springs, CO 80909

©2013 Product Concept Mfg., Inc. All rights reserved.

Written and Compiled by Patricia Mitchell
in association with Product Concept Mfg., Inc.

All scripture quotations are from the King James version
of the Bible unless otherwise noted.

Scriptures taken from the Holy Bible,
New International Version®, NIV®.
Copyright © 1973, 1978, 1984 by Biblica, Inc.™
Used by permission of Zondervan.
All rights reserved worldwide.
www.zondervan.com

Sayings not having a credit listed are contributed by writers
for Product Concept Mfg., Inc. or in a rare case,
the author is unknown.

Quick Little Devotions

The function of prayer
is not to influence God,
but rather to change the nature
of the one who prays.

Søren Kierkegaard

Leisurely mornings spent in quiet reflection...restful evenings devoted to meditation and prayer...dream on, right? That's a far cry from what your life's really like! Yet you're serious about exploring your heart's world, nurturing your spiritual gifts, and strengthening your relationship with God.

This book is designed with people just like you in mind—active, busy, engaged with life, and spiritually minded. With a thought-provoking quotation, a meaningful reflection, and little prayer to say, you can begin or end your day with God—or spend a quiet moment with Him whenever you need a word of encouragement and affirmation.

Pick up *Quick Little Devotions* for a simple way to make a big difference in your day, every day!

So Very Funny

Humor brings insight and tolerance.
Agnes Repplier

Who knows how to make you laugh? That person possesses a priceless gift. Humor keeps you from taking things—including yourself—way, way too seriously! It broadens your perspective so you can see the silly side of life. It shrinks your problems down to size, because a deep-down belly laugh gets you feeling that life is pretty good after all.

Perhaps you're not a natural-born comedian, but you have what it takes to cultivate a healthy, joyful sense of humor. It begins with a willingness to accept life without fear so you can relax and enjoy it. You'll find that humor, like a sparkly ribbon, weaves through your days as you respond to foolishness with a friendly chuckle... tweak an assumption with a well-placed quip...get a discussion back on track with a lighthearted word.

Joy of heart is a God-given gift, and from joy comes genuine humor, healing laughter, and the great delight of being able to share it with others.

Put joy into my heart, Dear God,
and grant me the gift of godly humor. Amen

The Power of Patience

Be patient toward all that is unsolved in your heart.
Rainer Maria Rilke

When something troubles you, you're restless until you resolve the issue. Whether it's by turning the matter over and over in your mind or talking about it with others, you want to find a solution. You want to get some answers, because you won't have peace until you do.

Patience! That's not a word we want to hear, but it's often the one we need to hear. It takes patience to not rely on assumptions, but dig for the facts...not settle for easy answers, but work toward the best answer... not jump to false conclusions, but wait for the truth to reveal itself.

Well-thought-out plans and considered solutions prove far more reliable than immediate answers. Knowledgeable speakers are respected, unlike misinformed chatterboxes. Lasting peace of mind comes when you're willing to be patient with yourself, others, and everything that's happening around you.

God-given patience is strength, and it's well worth the wait.

Dear God, enable me to wait patiently in all things. Amen

A Brand New Day

This is the day which the LORD hath made;
we will rejoice and be glad in it.
Psalm 118:24

When you wake tomorrow morning, imagine yourself standing at the door of the home of your dearest friend. You knock on the door, hear footsteps, and smile as the door opens and you're invited in. You don't know everything your friend has in mind to tell you this day, but whatever it is, you're delighted to listen and share.

Similarly, every morning you stand at the door of a brand new day. You're invited in. Greet the hours ahead as you would a dear friend. Although you don't know everything the day has in store for you—what it may show you, reveal to you, teach you, or give you—you're happy to have the privilege of being a part of it.

A day is a blessing from God, and He does not send you into it alone. Like a dear friend, He's there with you and for you. Lean on His guidance, comfort, and strength. Bring Him your gratitude for the hours. Share the gladness of every moment.

Dear God, thank You for the beginning of this day. Amen

A Real Difference

A kind heart is a fountain of gladness,
making everything in its vicinity freshen into smiles.
Washington Irving

Has someone's simple kindness ever brightened your day? Maybe it was a clerk who went out of her way to help you...a friend who dropped you a note just to say hello...a stranger who held the door open for you. What small, seemingly insignificant things, yet what a big difference they can make!

Your simple kindnesses do the same thing for others. You may never know that the few minutes you spent listening to someone filled a heart with renewed hope...the seemingly minor help you provided a person lifted a heavy burden from tired shoulders...the encouragement you gave a youngster filled her with hope and confidence.

Many people have grand ideas about what they could do to make a difference in the world if only they had the time, money, and influence. But each person who practices simple kindness is doing it every day, day in and day out.

Dear God, send me many opportunities today
to practice simple kindness. Amen

Excellent Choice

The strongest principle of growth lies in human choice.
George Eliot

Every choice we make reveals our desires and perceptions. Where we have options, the one we pick reflects our beliefs and values. When there's no feasible option, our choice to accept what's available is also a telling choice. How we elect to spend our time, money, and resources tells us a lot about ourselves and who we are.

If you want to know more about yourself, keep track of what you do with your time and money. Jot down the topics that occupy your thoughts and dreams. Where you have several available choices, ask yourself why you choose what you do. You may be pleasantly surprised at your ability to choose well, or you might discover places where you could learn to choose a little better.

The best choice of all is to spend time with God every day. Let Him guide you as you choose what's best for you.

Dear God, guide my thoughts and actions
so that I may learn to choose well. Amen

Well Said

Set a watch, O LORD, before my mouth;
keep the door of my lips.
Psalm 141:3

Contrary to a schoolyard saying about sticks and stones, words can hurt! They wound feelings, break hearts, and sever relationships. Words can echo in our thoughts for years, if not decades. As powerful as they are, however, words are what we use to talk about everything from today's weather to our deepest needs. We open our mouths, and words pour out!

Today, pay special attention to the words you say. Listen to your own voice as you speak to your loved ones, your friends, and the people you meet. Are these the words you would want to hear from others? Is your tone of voice warm and inviting? Are the echoes your words leave behind pleasant, uplifting, and encouraging?

When God's compassion, understanding, and wisdom fill your heart, the words that flow from your lips take on added strength and sweetness. With Him as its source, your voice blesses the world with His love.

Dear God, make me aware of the power of my words.
Enable me to bless others with the things I say. Amen

Content with Everything

I am always content with what happens;
for I know that what God chooses
is better than what I choose.
Epictetus

If you are content with what you have, it doesn't mean you don't desire to improve your circumstances or work to achieve a better tomorrow. On the contrary, contentment is active. It finds plenty to be thankful for wherever it finds itself. Though there are plans for the future, contentment never sacrifices the present moment to indulge in gloom, greed, or restlessness.

God has a plan for your life, and where you are right now is part of it. If you're struggling through hardship, He will bring you through it, perhaps to a place where you'll find fulfillment beyond your expectations. No challenge you face is a random accident, but something designed to strengthen you in heart and mind. What's not to your choosing might be exactly what God has chosen to nurture your spiritual growth.

Today, wish to be who you are, where you are, and with the people around you. Actively rest content with everything.

Thank You, dear God, for the gift of contentment
each day of my life. Amen

More Than You Know

I can do all this through him who gives me strength.
Philippians 4:13 NIV

Has your own courage, resilience, or perseverance ever surprised you? Think of the most difficult thing you've ever been through. If someone had told you beforehand that you would emerge a stronger person, you wouldn't have believed it. "Not me," you would have replied, "because that's something I just couldn't handle." When it came your way, however, you did—much to your own astonishment.

Your ability to meet and defeat life's troubles comes from God's power at work in you. When you bring your difficulties to Him in prayer, you are recognizing that you can't handle things on your own. He never intended that you should! As you seek His guidance and direction, the path through becomes clearer. When you put your faith in His strength, you discover more strength within you than you ever thought possible.

Surprise yourself! Tackle what you think you can't handle. Take on the power God has given you, because you have more know-how, strength, and survival sense than you imagine.

Dear God, show me how to use the strength
You have given to me. Amen

Love's Foundation

Love does not consist in gazing at each other,
but in looking outward in the same direction.
Antoine de Saint-Exupéry

Whether between lovers, friends, or family members, love requires a strong foundation. Love is sure to end in disappointment if it's based on sentiment or romanticism, and it won't last long if it's spoiled by criticism. Certainly negativity and self-centeredness are poor roots if we expect love to blossom.

Ask long-married couples for their secret, and you're likely to hear them say that their love's foundation is mutual trust and respect. The same holds true for all stable and healthy relationships. Even a casual friendship would fade if you could neither trust nor respect the person!

Trust and respect makes a good foundation for a loving relationship with God, too. Spiritual feelings and emotional highs come and go, but trust and respect get stronger. You can depend on His love, even if you stumble. You can honor His divine will, even though you don't always understand it. Your relationship with God is one of thriving, ever-blooming love.

Thank You, dear God, for the bond of love between us! Amen

Just a Feeling

One's feelings waste themselves in words;
they ought all to be distilled into actions which bring results.
Florence Nightingale

There's something you know better than anyone else:
Your own feelings. Not emotions, but your gut reactions.
Your instincts. Your intuition. Yet, if you're like many
people, you hesitate to let intuition guide your decisions
or even enter into the conversation. Fear of criticism,
frustration at being overruled so many times in the past,
and lack of self-confidence play a part in dismissing the
voice of intuition.

Perhaps you can think back to a time you went ahead
and acted against your feelings, and then later discovered you were right all along. If only you had spoken
up...if only you had insisted upon being heard...if only
you had acted on your better judgment! But what a
valuable lesson you learned. Now when your intuition
speaks, you listen and you act.

Some might even say that a well-honed intuition is
the voice of God speaking in the human heart. Maybe it
is. All the more reason to pay close attention to it.

Dear God, enable me to stand up for the way I feel,
even if it goes against what others are saying. Amen

A Happy Duty

There is no duty we so much underrate
as the duty of being happy.
Robert Louis Stevenson

If you have never thought of being happy as a duty, think about it now. Instead of happiness as the icing on the cake, call it the whole cake. If you keep a to-do list, put "be happy" at the very top. It's your duty, remember!

You might say you don't have what it takes to be happy—perfect body...perfect home...perfect relationships...perfect life. But you're old enough to know that you don't live in a perfect world. You have better! God has blessed you with your own personality, thoughts, hopes, and aspirations. He has given you the capacity to work toward your dreams and encourage others to reach for theirs. You're able to remember good times and look forward to more. You can solve problems and overcome challenges. You can feel, love, laugh, touch, and care.

Best of all, you have a God who loves you and who calls you into a relationship with Him. Now how do you feel about doing your duty today?

Dear God, thank You for all the reasons I have to be happy.

Amen

Risky Business

The fishermen know that the sea is dangerous
and the storm terrible, but they have never found these dangers
sufficient reason for remaining ashore.
Vincent van Gogh

There are risks, and there are risks. Sometimes people take highly ill-advised risks that land them in places they don't want to be. That's no reason to avoid taking risks, but a reason to take only well-thought-out, calculated risks. Of course, no amount of planning can guarantee a good outcome—that's why it's call risky!

Taking even a calculated risk is about as comfortable as stepping off the edge of a cliff. Making the leap, though, can bring huge rewards. How else can you reach your full potential unless you get out of your comfort zone? And even if the risk you take doesn't work out, you've gained experience in the process.

Wherever your risks have taken you or will take you, God is there. If you fall, He's there to pick you up. If you reach your star, He's there to guide you to the next and the next and beyond. Risk it!

Dear God, guide me when my next step
requires that I take a risk. Amen

Path to Success

Let no feeling of discouragement prey upon you,
and in the end you are sure to succeed.
Abraham Lincoln

"If at first you don't succeed, try, try again." To the time-honored piece of advice, one wit has added "but to keep trying the same thing is insanity!" Without a doubt, some things aren't going to work, at least for the present. But get discouraged? No!

You're unlikely to reach any worthwhile goal without struggle, set-backs, and continued effort. Some actions you take might not pan out or may prove unproductive, but that's all part of learning what works and what doesn't. Approached from another direction, your objective gets closer and your next steps clearer. The know-how you get from trying and trying again (in different ways!) is invaluable, and you can gain it by no other means.

If you're feeling discouraged, a new way of trying can bring you closer to your goal. Perhaps another approach will open a whole new path for you to follow. Try...always try, for in the end you'll succeed in everything God has planned for you.

Grant me the motivation to try again, dear God,
whenever I feel discouraged. Amen

Soul-Deep Peace

Peace I leave with you, my peace I give unto you.
John 14:27

The peace that God gives those who put their faith in Him has nothing to do with what's going on in the world. For sure, if we had to wait until everything in the world calms down before we could know peace, we'd never glimpse even a moment's peace!

But God's peace is a strong, steady, soul-deep peace. It comes to you when you place your trust in Him and His wisdom, knowing that all things—no matter how frightening, upsetting, or destructive—lie under His control. Though circumstances may do their best to wear you down, they cannot disturb your peace in knowing your God's presence. He helps, comforts, and strengthens you, and nothing can change His love for you.

Frightening news and terrifying events have no power to shatter your inner peace when it's God's peace you possess in your mind, heart, and soul. Understand it? No; it's beyond human understanding. But bask in it? Absolutely yes!

Dear God, grant me peace as only You can give. Amen

Gratitude How-To

Gratitude is the fruit of great cultivation.
Samuel Johnson

We're often admonished to "be thankful," and we admit, yes, we should be thankful. With a brief nod to God, however, we're right back to the same old feelings—thankful in words, but not in truth. We see someone comfortably well-off, and we wonder why we have to struggle so. Sure, we have a lot to be thankful for, yet...

Perhaps what's missing is how to be thankful—the recognition that gratitude doesn't come naturally, but needs nurturing and cultivation before it can flower. You grow in gratitude as you embrace the present moment and savor all the fun, funny, exciting, and beautiful things around you. While you may need to make a special point of noticing your blessings at first, soon thankfulness becomes part of you. Without anyone's prompting, you'll be truly thankful.

As an added bonus, you know whom to thank. Let God in on everything you're thankful for, because every giver welcomes a word of gratitude!

Thank You, God, for everything! Amen

Traits to Tweak

The greater part of our happiness or misery
depends on our dispositions and not on our circumstances.
Martha Washington

Perhaps we're born with a particular temperament—
fretful or cheerful, apprehensive or easy-going. But as we
grow older and more self-aware, we're able to accentuate
the positive side of our personality and curb our less
helpful traits. We discover, for example, that constant
anxiety prevents us from appreciating the good things
in life, so we consciously turn off the worry machine. If
stress becomes the order of the day, we find a relaxation
technique that works for us so we can rest.

Your temperament matters, because it shapes your
self-image, interactions with others, and sense of satisfaction in life. It affects how productively you handle
problems and how well you're able to rise above difficult
circumstances.

If your temperament needs a little tweaking, why not
make some changes? Think about the characteristic
that seems to so naturally, but just isn't working
for you. Remember, you have a God-given ability that
trumps anything else—you can choose to change.

Dear God, help me make changes so I can follow
the way you have laid out for me. Amen

Everything's Going Your Way

In prosperity, when the stream of life flows
in accordance with our wishes,
let us diligently avoid all arrogance,
haughtiness, and pride.
Cicero

Though we may feel weak when we're going through tough times, we're actually strong and growing stronger. When misfortune strikes, we're more apt to think through our actions and decisions, and accept help from the people around us. In the process, endurance and self-confidence build up, and our trust in the goodwill of others increases.

When everything's going our way, however, we feel strong, but we're most in danger of weakness—the weakness of thinking that we're entirely self-made, we need no one else, and we deserve our status, wealth, fame, or good fortune. Any one of these thoughts deserves a red flag!

God blesses you with many extraordinary gifts designed to bring you strength, not weakness. It is great strength to remember where your good fortune comes from, to share your gifts with others, and to bless as many people as you can and as generously as God has blessed you.

Dear God, when everything's going my way,
grant me wisdom, understanding, and generosity. Amen

Just As You Are

Everyone must row with the oars they have.
Proverb

If you're like many people, there are things about yourself that you wish you could change. Perhaps you'd like to be taller or shorter, darker or fairer, or more in appearance or advantages like a person you admire. While someone else's example may inspire you to make positive changes, one thing remains the same: You are who you are—and thank God!

Yes, thank God, because the way He formed you was no whim or accident. He gave you certain physical and emotional attributes so you could best fulfill His purpose for your life. That doesn't mean everything about you is perfect, because you were not born into a perfect world; but it does mean everything about you is right for who you are and where you are.

Anyone have a problem with your God-given self? If so, remember whose problem it isn't—yours!

Dear God, help me accept myself and others for who we are:
Your beloved daughters and sons. Amen

Obviously a Pleasure

*Be glad of life because it gives you the chance to love
and to work and to play and to look up at the stars.*
Henry van Dyke

"So what are you going to do about it?" someone
might ask when we're noodling over how to approach a
problem. Rarely will you hear a question like that about
pleasure! After all, the answer's obvious: Enjoy it!

Yet what's so obvious when it comes to pleasures like
vacations, celebrations, or meeting friends isn't so clear
when we're talking about life. Just life, which includes
the pleasure of being able to breathe, think, feel, touch,
imagine, and dream. The pleasure of savoring taste
and fragrance, and the pleasure of discovering more
about people and places and possibilities. And don't
forget the pleasure of losing yourself in a good book...
of sensing God's presence through great music, art, and
architecture...of looking up into a starry night sky and
marveling at His glorious creation.

Today, what's your pleasure? Whatever it may be, do
something about it, because pleasure comes with the
incomparable privilege of being alive!

**Dear God, I cannot thank You enough
for the pleasure and privilege of life! Amen**

Your Good Servant

If you would have a faithful servant,
and one that you like, serve yourself.
Benjamin Franklin

There are things no one can do for us. While other people may provide invaluable help and support when we're facing serious struggles or up against challenging times, they can go with us only so far. The finish is up to us.

Example: A friend can offer us a shoulder to cry on, but she isn't responsible for stepping in and solving our problem. That's our job! A dietician can provide us with a plan for healthy eating, but we have to carry it out in our daily choices before we can have any benefit. A counselor can help us discover a good way to deal with our circumstances, but no one else can actually make new behavior a reality except ourselves.

Even God doesn't do for you what you can do for yourself. Instead, He assures you of His presence, and He gives you certain physical, spiritual, and material resources. Yes, He's given you a good and capable servant at your beck and call—yourself.

Dear God, grant me the self-reliance it takes
to tackle my problems and challenges. Amen

Head and Heart

A wise man should have money in his head,
but not in his heart.
Jonathan Swift

Whether we're rolling in dollars or barely making ends meet, money is more than likely to pose huge problems. If we have a lot of money, it easily emerges as our source of identity and security. Then the more money we get, the more worthwhile we feel.

If we're on a tight budget, money poses an obvious problem, and we find ourselves just as obsessed with getting more money as our wealthy counterpart. In a desperate attempt to pay our bills and meet our obligations, we neglect the fact that God provides. We forget His power to the point that we don't even ask Him for help! For the poor, the rich, and everyone in between, money exerts enormous control over our daily thoughts and actions—if we let it.

Today, talk to God about money. He won't be shocked. Ask Him how you can spend, save, and share your money so that it stays where it belongs—in your head, not in your heart.

Dear God, help me cultivate a healthy
and positive attitude toward money. Amen

Live Performance

*Life is like playing a violin in public
and learning the instrument as one goes on.*
Samuel Butler

Not one of us gets a practice run at life! Instead, we're forced to make our decisions as each day comes. Even if we have some prior experience to rely on, there's no guarantee that things will turn out the same as last time. Sure, we can do our best, but....

If the thought makes you tremble a little, look at it this way: You have reached where you are in life now largely because of the decisions you have made. Some were good ones and some could have been better. Through it all, however, God has brought you to this time and this place. He has walked with you through both tough times and great times. Will He stay with you now as you grapple with today's decisions? Of course He will.

Every human decision comes with an element of serendipity. But God's willingness and ability to uphold you never wavers. His love is always for sure, now and forever.

**In all my decisions, dear God,
grant me trust in Your continuing care. Amen**

Curiosity Comes Calling

I think, at a child's birth,
if a mother could ask a fairy godmother
to endow it with the most useful gift,
that gift should be curiosity.
Eleanor Roosevelt

As children, we're not afraid to ask questions. We like to learn things, and we take great pleasure in knowing things. But as we grow older, curiosity about the world often wanes. What we don't know, we think, can't hurt us!

But it can. Perhaps not the thing itself, but our lack of curiosity can seriously hurt us. When we find ourselves saying, "I don't care"...when we immediately reject new developments...when we summarily refuse to consider a point of view other than our own, we're letting our sense of curiosity slip away. We're giving up a God-given gift that keeps us alert, interested, and interesting in favor of a self-centered attitude.

It's worth whatever it takes to keep curiosity alive, and it really doesn't take much. All it requires for curiosity to come calling is a willingness to ask a question... to wonder about a mystery...to discover something new...to explore another point of view.

Thank You, dear God, for the gift of curiosity.
Never let me neglect to use it! Amen

People Watching

Nothing is so infectious as an example.
François de La Rochefoucauld

People are watching! Even though you're not standing in front of a classroom or speaking in front of large audiences, people notice how you talk, act, move, and gesture. Your words and behavior influence others, especially those closest to you. You've heard it said that children learn more by example than by speeches, and the same holds true for everyone. Yes, people are watching!

Your everyday example of patience and kindness, friendliness and helpfulness, goodwill and consideration mean more than anything you could say about yourself. Even strangers who cross your path sense the kind of person you are by the way you carry yourself, speak to others, and react to your surroundings. Poise, self-confidence, and a smile convey the image of someone others would like to know.

Yes, we learn from parents, teachers, mentors, leaders, and role models, but it's possible that we learn more simply from watching each other.

Dear God, grant me the privilege of setting a good example
in the things I do and say. Amen

Great Things

Keep away from people who try to belittle your ambitions.
Small people always do that, but the really great
make you feel that you, too, can become great.
Mark Twain

When you share your inmost thoughts and private hopes with another person, you're extending a precious gift—the gift of your trust. You trust them not to make fun of you or laugh at your ideas. You confide in them, expecting them to honor your life-affirming aspirations and support you in your efforts to make your good dreams come true.

Though God knows the thoughts that fill your heart, He invites you to confide in Him. Trust Him with your deepest secrets, even those you may never have had the courage to tell anyone else. Don't worry! He will never disparage you or make you feel small, no matter how seemingly out of reach your ambition appears right now.

What is it? Whisper your words in God's ear. Hear His as He reaches out to you with wisdom and understanding. Let Him open the way to great things for you.

I trust You, dear God, with all my hopes and dreams. Amen

Practical Matters

To know what has to be done, then do it,
comprises the whole philosophy of practical life.
William Osler

In some situations, we don't know what to do next; but in most, we do. We have an accurate idea of the action necessary to get the task done...the work completed...the goal achieved. Trouble is, we really don't want to do it.

In the course of your day, how many things fall into this category? If the list is long, perhaps it's time to take a look at what's on the list. You probably can find several tasks you might not want to do, but it's not practical to leave them undone. But maybe there are some items you can check off your list—things you do out of habit or simply because you've always done it.

Without question is the practical matter of your spiritual walk. You know what you need to do, and you may not feel like doing it every day. That's why it's no shame to ask God for inspiration and motivation as you move forward on your spiritual journey.

Dear God, enable me to do everything I can
to grow and mature in faith. Amen

The God He Is

Let us therefore come boldly unto the throne of grace,
that we may obtain mercy,
and find grace to help in time of need.
Hebrews 4:16

Stern judge. Fearsome force. All-seeing examiner. Certainly God is all these things, but some people believe He's only those things. Afraid of His anger, they want to cover up, not confess, their weaknesses. Terrified He'll punish them, they definitely don't feel comfortable coming to Him in prayer.

But God is more, much more. A judge, yes, but a judge full of mercy who yearns to soothe the hurting soul and heal the broken heart. A fearsome force, yes, but a force for life, for love, for good. An all-seeing examiner, yes, but an examiner who looks with the eyes of compassion and understanding.

Can you go to God in prayer? Yes. Imagine yourself approaching Him, touching His sleeve, and receiving His kindly attention. Feel the comfort of His embrace, hear the lilt of His laughter, and see the twinkle in His eye. That's the kind of God He is.

Thank You, dear God, for being the loving God that You are.
Amen

Dark and Light

We do not live an equal life,
but one of contrasts and patchwork;
now a little joy, then a sorrow,
now a sin, then a generous or brave action.
Ralph Waldo Emerson

If you look at a well-designed patchwork quilt, you'll notice that the maker mixes light- and dark-colored fabrics. To appreciate the overall design, you need to stand back. Only then can you appreciate the beauty of the quilt.

In a similar way, your life is sprinkled with light, bright times when everything goes along splendidly. Then come darker times with setbacks, challenges, and disappointments. If you focus exclusively on either the light times or the dark times, however, you will miss the beauty of your years. It's the good and the bad, the celebrations and the sorrows, the wins and the losses that make up the design of a full, fulfilling, and beautiful life.

Let God, who knows all your days, enable you to stand back and look at all the times of your life. When all you can see is darkness, let Him show you the light.

Dear God, help me appreciate all the times of my life. Amen

Spiritual Maturity

Be not afraid of growing slowly,
be afraid only of standing still.
Proverb

Spiritual growth comes slowly, and it develops over a lifetime. Even the most spiritually mature didn't get that way in a day or a year, but over the course of decades. Empowered by God's Spirit at work in their hearts and minds, they plumbed the depths of Scripture. They prayed about it and meditated on its meaning for their lives. Most importantly, they applied it.

Maturity in spiritual matters develops not when we're filled with lofty notions, but only when we press our heavenly thoughts into an earthly purpose. That takes time! Each stage of life brings more opportunities to apply a deeper understanding of God's will and His ways to evermore complex situations. As we persevere in work and in prayer, we gradually grow in spiritual maturity.

God's Spirit is at work in you, because you're thinking of God and probing His will and His ways. Keep going, and keep growing in spiritual maturity as you apply what you're learning to your daily life.

Keep me growing, dear God,
in spiritual knowledge and wisdom. Amen

In the Mirror

You can't depend on your eyes
when your imagination is out of focus.
Mark Twain

Have you ever stood in front of a funhouse mirror? If so, you know what it's like to see yourself completely differently—pulled ten feet tall or stretched nine feet wide! It's all for laughs, of course. So how about something just as lighthearted, but with a serious thought attached?

Today, try seeing yourself and everyone else differently. If you usually feel timid, see yourself confident. Would it help to stand in front of the confidence mirror? How would you look? How would you act? If you generally walk around with furrowed brows, pose in front of the serenity mirror. Look at yourself! Do you like what you see? And then have everyone else walk past the lovable mirror...the God's-child mirror...the I-understand-you mirror. Don't you see them differently than you did before?

There's no trick, though, in how God sees you. With His own eyes, He looks at you with all-encompassing love, and that will never lose its shape!

Dear God, enable me to see the world through Your eyes. Amen

Exceed Expectations

Dream lofty dreams, and as you dream, so shall you become.
Your vision is the promise of what you shall at last unveil.
John Ruskin

Most managers in the workplace give each employee a periodic performance review. Generally the quality of an employee's work falls into one of several categories ranging from "does not meet expectations" (uh-oh) to "exceeds expectations" (yay).

Today, why not give your hopes and dreams an imaginary performance review? Just how are the thoughts you have about your future working for you? Do they excite you? If not, perhaps it's time to show them the door and make room for newer, fresher ideas that thrill the person you have become.

Do your hopes and dreams inspire you to aim for them, and are you taking practical steps to make them come true? If you're not motivated to do anything but think about them, they're just taking up space in your head!

Invite big, lofty, God-quality hopes and dreams to come and work for you. You'll like the way they perform. They'll exceed your expectations, and help you do the same!

Dear God, enlarge my expectations,
because with You, nothing is impossible. Amen

The Big Search

Nothing gives rest but the sincere search for truth.
Blaise Pascal

Who's searching for whom? When we turn to God in prayer or open the pages of Scripture, we may believe that we're looking for God. When we visit a church or immerse ourselves in the beauty of nature, we may say we're visiting where God lives. It's us, we think, on a quest for the divine.

But it's God on a quest for the human—us. When we stray from His path, He comes to rescue us the way a good shepherd would go after a lost sheep. Though a single person is one among billions of people, He values each one of us as a poverty-stricken woman would value a single small coin. Not one is unneeded.

Go ahead, though, and seek God. Find Him in Scripture, in worship, and in nature. Discover Him in love and laughter and friendship. Just remember that while you're searching, He has already found you!

Thank You, dear God, for searching for me! Amen

From the Heart

There is no happiness in having or in getting, but only in giving.
Henry Drummond

What is love? Poets have spilled oceans of ink on the question from earliest times up to the present day! But God, who is love, chose not to tell us, but show us. So He gave us life and breath, gave us His Son Jesus, and gave us forgiveness, kindness, compassion, and understanding. According to God, love is giving.

The greatest love you can show anyone is the gift of yourself. That means giving your time and attention not only to your friends, but to people who try your patience...listening not only to those who agree with you, but to those who challenge your way of thinking...welcoming not only the newcomer who looks like you, but the one who's different in appearance and background...loving not only the lovable, but the unlovable, too.

What is love? It's more than sublime words, more than fancy gifts, more than anything money can buy. Real love is God-style love—giving from the heart.

Dear God, grant me the power to show my love
by giving of myself to others. Amen

Grow Through It

Adversity has the effect of eliciting talents
which in prosperous circumstances would have lain dormant.
Horace

Adverse circumstances may come into your life, but no matter what they are, you are not your circumstances. See the difference? If you let your circumstances define you, you're hooking your identity onto something about as firm as a leaf in the wind. Circumstances change!

Perhaps the difficult circumstances you're in right now will leave you in a far different place physically, emotionally, and mentally than you were before, but they will pass. Time sees to that, and time never fails. What lasts is your God-given identity His dear daughter...His dear son. No situation can take that away, so why hide it beneath layers of other labels? Why accept any other definition of you?

All circumstances, especially difficult ones, are meant to go through and grow through, with God's help and strength. They're designed to show you who you are, not define who you are. Your circumstances aren't you—you are you!

Dear God, keep me as your beloved one
as I go through all the circumstances of my life. Amen

Miracles All Around

To me every hour of the light and dark is a miracle,
every cubic inch of space is a miracle.
Walt Whitman

Someone once said that miracles are seen only by those who believe in them. How true! For those who discount miracles, the stricken patient's inexplicable recovery is called luck. When they find themselves at the right time and place, it's coincidence. The events in their lives fall under one umbrella—destiny.

How about you? God is capable of miracles, and they happen all the time. Are your eyes open to them? If so, you know that God, according to His will, touches you with His hand of comfort and healing, forgiveness and peace...puts you where you need to be so you can receive the blessings He has in store for you...guides you all your days so you can fulfill His good and gracious plans for you.

Luck? Coincidence? Destiny? Those words might describe it for some, but we have another word we like to use—miracle.

Dear God, thank You for all the miracles
You continue to work in my life! Amen

Opportunity Knocks

The opportunity that God sends
does not wake up those who are asleep.
Proverb

Opportunity knocks, but we don't always hear it. Are we expecting it to crash the door down? Opportunity rarely does that! More often than not, opportunity comes with a light rap or even a slight rustle of movement just beyond our line of vision. And not just one opportunity, but scads of opportunities; not just once in a lifetime, but daily.

Yes, daily. Today there's the opportunity to put on a smile, pay a compliment, help a friend, and see the sunny side of life. You have the opportunity to feel good about yourself, think healthy and life-affirming thoughts, work to the best of your ability, and make a couple changes for the better. Opportunity knocks, inviting you to ponder a question, solve a problem, fix something broken, and learn something new.

God knocks, too. Open the door to time with Him, to prayer, to faith, to trust. Like opportunity, He knocks not just once in a lifetime, but every day.

Open my ears, dear God, so that I hear You
when You knock! Amen

Pardon and Peace

You can't undo anything you've already done,
but you can face up to it. You can tell the truth.
You can seek forgiveness. And then let God do the rest.
Tertullian

No one enjoys acknowledging mistakes! Life's blunders make us feel like bumbling fools. But, red face and all, we apologize, make amends where we can, and keep moving forward (although with a little more savvy than we had before).

Deep inside your heart, however, you might hear a whisper telling you that there's something missing. It comes as a nagging feeling that, despite all you've done, you haven't quite gotten to the core of the matter. What's lacking? An admission before God, along with a prayerful request for His pardon.

With God comes not only forgiveness, but peace of mind in knowing that you can truly put the matter behind you. It's gone from His eyes! His pardon brings you the confidence you need to go forward, relying on His Spirit to help you avoid that same mistake. But if you stumble again? He forgives—again and again. Just ask Him!

Thank You, dear God, for the assurance
of Your pardon and peace. Amen

Something to See

People look at the outward appearance,
but the LORD looks at the heart.
1 Samuel 16:7 NIV

We know we're not supposed to judge by appearance, but we do. When we're meeting people for the first time, we can't help but draw certain conclusions from the way they dress, act, and speak. As we get to know them better, we might discover that we've been absolutely right all along...or completely wrong from the start.

With God, outward appearances mean nothing. When your heavenly Father looks at you, He looks inside your heart. He sees your struggles and your fears, and He soothes you with His comfort and encouragement. He's aware of your good intentions and motivations, even if they have been misinterpreted by others. He knows the person you are deep down inside, and He discerns the beauty there.

Appearances matter only to those looking on the outside. God, who examines your heart, sees the real you—one of His wonderful creations...His beloved child.

Look on me with love, dear God! Amen

No Question About It

*Doubt is the vestibule through which all must pass
before they can enter into the temple of wisdom.*
Charles Caleb Colton

When you doubt something, you have an incentive to investigate further. To ask more questions. To delve deeper into the matter. To find out for yourself whether your doubts are justified. But if you never follow up on your doubts, you have no hope of ever discovering the truth.

Many people are afraid to express their doubts about spiritual matters. They may question things they've been taught as children or have misgivings concerning what a pastor has said, but they don't ask for clarification. They never probe for an explanation that they can get their minds around. Is it any wonder they're never quite sure what they believe?

Doubts work against you if you let them hold you in uncertainty. Doubts work for you, however, when they're a springboard to a deeper understanding and increased appreciation of spiritual truths. Your doubts are simply important questions waiting to be asked.

**Dear God, lead me to a deeper understanding of your truth.
Amen**

So to Speak

*The nearer you come into relation with a person,
the more necessary do tact and courtesy become.*
Oliver Wendell Holmes

In all relationships, especially close ones, there are times when we're compelled to bring up a difficult topic. It's time for a parent to turn in the car keys...for a spouse to handle money more responsibly...for an adult child to face the consequences of her actions...for a friend who is contemplating a risky course of action. Those are uncomfortable conversations to open with someone we love and care about!

Precisely because we love and care about the person, we think deeply before speaking. A blunt statement of the truth rarely spurs thoughtful discussion, but tact and courtesy spare feelings, respect a person's dignity, and ease the way to a productive and effective conversation.

And most important? Prayer. Pray that you will convey God's compassion, understanding, and kindness to the person you love, and the words will take care of themselves.

**Enable me to speak Your words of love,
especially in difficult situations. Amen**

Something New

All life is an experiment.
The more experiments you make, the better.
Ralph Waldo Emerson

If you keep houseplants, you know what happens when a plant has been in the same pot for too long. It gets root bound! Lift the plant from its pot, and you see a wall of tangled roots wrapped around and around the hard, packed soil. The plant needs a bigger container if you want it to keep growing.

You get root bound, too, when you do the same things day in and day out. There comes a point where you're not growing anymore because routine has you stuck in a rut. How about fixing the problem? Shake free of the old soil and try something new! A varied route to work. Another restaurant, movie, book, or vacation spot. Anything different!

A spiritual rut can hinder you, too. Talk about spiritual things with friends. Read the spiritual classics. Ponder new questions. Seek deep answers. If you feel root bound, give yourself room to expand and keep growing!

Dear God, help me find new opportunities to grow and flourish.

Amen

Growing in the Process

I am not bound to succeed,
but I am bound to live up to what light I have.
Abraham Lincoln

There's no such thing as assured success! Yet we often work toward our goals that way, believing that if we don't get positive results from our efforts, we have failed. But even if we haven't ended up where we had hoped, we have gained more than we have lost. We have given the goal our best effort, and we've grown in the process.

We've been blessed with a dream, and we planned how we might bring it to reality. Along the way, we learned how to persevere in the face of inevitable hindrances and how to cope with unexpected difficulties. By challenging ourselves to reach beyond today's capabilities, we cultivated and tested the skills we need for a better tomorrow.

What you can do is second to what you can dream. Though there's no assurance you'll succeed in making each dream come true, there's every assurance that in giving it your best effort, you'll succeed in living life to the fullest!

Dear God, guide my efforts and help me
Give my best to all I do. Amen

All You Need

I care not so much what I am to others as what I am to myself.
I will be rich by myself, and not by borrowing.
Michel de Montaigne

It's natural to describe ourselves as son, daughter, sister, brother, wife, husband. Sometimes we point with pride to the fact that we're friends with this person or associated with that company. But ultimately, the most important relationship is the one we have with ourselves.

Even if you have connections that earn you a place in the society pages or on national TV, there's no substitute for a healthy, God-given sense of self-worth. With God, you don't need anyone else's limelight to make you shine! His Spirit in your heart gives you all the glow you need. Sure, your relationships matter and they give you a certain identity in the world. They put you as a particular person in a particular place among particular people. Thank God for His good and gracious gift of human relationships!

But you are more than your relationships. Within yourself, you have all you need as a loved one of God, your heavenly Father.

Grant me the ability, dear God,
to know my own worth in Your eyes. Amen

Something to Think About

Could we change our attitude,
we should not only see life differently,
but life itself would come to be different.
Life would undergo a change of appearance
because we ourselves had undergone a change in attitude.
Katherine Mansfield

More than we realize, our thoughts create our world. Unkind thoughts about others set us up to judge and criticize, and then our eyes are clouded with even more unkind thoughts. Through the fog of unkindness, nothing looks bright, appealing, or worth loving. Increasingly, our world becomes smaller and darker, all because of our thoughts.

When we think about others with compassion, however, we're primed to see their good points. We're apt to empathize, help where we can, and make a positive difference. Our kind thoughts leave us feeling good about others and about ourselves. The end result? The warmth and light of more kindly thoughts, more kindly actions!

If you feel the shadows of unkindness hovering over your heart and mind, remember God's love for you. He holds no unkind thoughts toward you. What's more, He has given you everything you need to shine the light of kindness on everyone around you.

Thank You, dear God, for loving me.
Help me share Your love with others. Amen

All About Fences

Don't ever take a fence down
until you know the reason why it was put up.
G. K. Chesterton

Walk through a zoo, and it's doubtful you'll hear anyone ask why there are fences around the lions' space or the bears' enclosure. Fences, of course, keep us separated from animals that could do us harm (and separate the animals from those among us who might annoy them with overly friendly hugs and nudges!).

Like fences, social rules and standards can separate people from one another, but they also can protect feelings, ease relationships, and guard privacy. For example, we like to tear down fences that cause us to distrust or misunderstand others. Yet fences that separate acceptable from unacceptable words and behavior work to protect the dignity of everyone. Those fences make it possible to live in community with all our neighbors.

When social standards or expectations stand between you and what you would like to do, step back. Prayerfully determine if it should be torn down, or if it's standing there for a God-pleasing reason.

Dear God, before I act against social norms,
grant me wisdom to know Your good and gracious will. Amen

Looking at Today

We are always paid for our suspicion
by finding what we suspect.
Henry David Thoreau

Things come that you'd just as soon go away, and things go that you wish would stay forever. It's all part of life's turning seasons. But if you focus only on the difficulties and the losses, you will miss the good things that time has brought to you.

Imagine you're holding a rose. Are you going to focus on the prickly thorns or the satiny petals? In the same way, examine the challenges you're facing. You can see them as insurmountable obstacles or life-affirming opportunities. Are losses in the picture? You can think of them as the cause of your gloom or as the reason you're thankful to have had the chance to experience good times, gladness, and love.

Change brings challenges and sorrows, defeats and disappointments. And at the same time it brings openings and opportunities, fresh possibilities and new promises. Today, are you looking at the roses or at the thorns?

Enable me, dear God,
to make the most of all I have today. Amen

A Relationship Worth Keeping

Happiness must be cultivated. It is like character.
It is not a thing to be safely let alone for a moment,
or it will run to weeds.
Elizabeth Stuart Phelps

Our relationships won't stay healthy, vibrant, and rewarding unless we make an effort to keep them that way. That's why we do things to please a spouse, show love to our children, and keep in touch with friends. We cherish those relationships, and would not want to lose them through neglect.

Happiness is like a relationship. When we fail to cultivate it, happiness drifts away. We may wait for it, hope for it, or even expect it, but happiness isn't a condition that drops from the sky on specially blessed people. Rather, it's cultivated much like a relationship. We make an effort to receive happiness by being open to it, by seeing the positive side of things, and by appreciating the blessings God has given us. We keep happiness by continuing to nurture it with optimism, gratitude, and positive thoughts and actions.

How healthy, vibrant, and rewarding is your relationship to happiness? It's a relationship well worth keeping!

Dear God, You are the source of all true happiness! Amen

God's Presence in You

*There is a God-shaped vacuum in the heart of every man
which cannot be filled by any created thing, but only by God.*
Blaise Pascal

No matter how much we possess, we're missing
something without God's presence in our lives. That's
because, try as we might, we can't fill our spiritual needs
with material things.

When God fills your spiritual needs, everything else
falls into place. Because God is able to meet your deepest
needs, all the rest—who you are, what you're doing, and
the people around you—take on new meaning. You're
able to enjoy the material blessings around you in a way
never before possible.

There's a place in you that only God can fill. Whether
you think of it as your soul or spirit or the inmost
depths of your heart, it's a place that belongs to Him.
Nothing anyone can give you or anything you can get on
your own compares to God at the center of your life.

Dear God, enter my heart and make it your home. Amen

A Cooling Conversation

Courage consists not in hazarding without fear,
but being resolutely minded in a just cause.
Plutarch

If someone says something offensive, you may find it hard to simply shrug it off. Yet if you let the comment simmer inside, it inevitably boils over into anger, bitterness, or retaliation. A relationship with the person becomes impossible. Your best course? As soon as possible, speak to the person who has offended us.

The person may not realize he has caused offense, and will apologize immediately. She may not think what she said was rude, and your insight will give her the awareness she needs. Maybe because of where he was coming from and where you were coming from, you thoroughly misread each other! You'll both be glad someone—you—had the courage to start talking.

Perhaps you find some things God says in Scripture to be hard to understand or even offensive. As always, the best course is to bring it out into the open. Pray about it. Discuss the matter with a pastor or mature Christian. Your relationship with God depends on it.

Dear God, grant me the courage to bring up and discuss
comments that bother me. Amen

A Necessary Good

*Nowhere can a man find a quieter
or more untroubled retreat than in his own soul.*
Marcus Aurelius

It's when you're most stressed that you feel you have less time to spend with God. There's so much to get done! There aren't enough hours in the day for the necessities, much less...

But wait. Just as necessary as food for the body...as needful as water for good health...is time with God for your soul. When you meditate on God's work in your life, give thanks for the blessings, and petition Him for your needs, you feed your heart and mind. You are taking time out for what's more necessary than all necessities, and that is your spiritual wellbeing.

God has given you many responsibilities, and you may feel overwhelmed as you tackle everything calling for your attention. In His love and understanding, however, He has provided a place where you can go each day for rest and restoration of body, mind, and soul. That's the place called your daily time with God, and it's a necessity.

Dear God, please refresh me with Your love. Amen

The Faith-Full Life

Faith is an excitement and an enthusiasm,
a state of intellectual magnificence
which we must not squander on our way through life.
George Sand

If your life has lost a bit of its spark lately, try this: Apply faith. Apply faith in God's love, care, and goodness to every hour, every circumstance, every feeling of the day!

Imagine waking in the morning full of anticipation for the day ahead. Because you have faith, no regrets from yesterday cloud your enthusiasm for the coming hours, and no fears of the future keep you from embracing whatever may lie before you. Imagine going through your day not worried or anxious, because faith tells you that God has everything under control.

Imagine knowing you have the strength to handle whatever might come your way because you have God's shoulder to lean on. Imagine what it would feel like to sleep peacefully each night, for you have loved, helped, forgiven, and given thanks this day.

Imagine! And with faith, it's possible to live a life of days sparkling with joy and fulfillment. It's possible to sleep nights resting in God-sent comfort and peace.

Dear God, fill my heart with joy-filled faith in You. Amen

Freedom of Control

He that hath no rule over his own spirit
is like a city that is broken down, and without walls.
Proverbs 25:28

Self-control isn't mentioned much anymore. You don't hear popular speakers talk about doing things in moderation or honoring God's guidance. In fact, many advocate the opposite. Free yourself! Express yourself! Do your own thing! Even some parents are reluctant to teach self-control for fear rules will hamper their children's development.

Yet we know that avoiding risky behaviors shields us from preventable hardships and difficulties. Steering clear of over-indulgence allows us to enjoy those things that God has meant as a blessing and a pleasure when used in moderation. Holding to time-honored rules frees us to pour our time and energy into activities that will work for our good and for the good of those around us.

Though self-control isn't the In Thing these days, this much is for sure: When God-given self-control rules your life, you possess true freedom.

Teach me, dear God, to curb my harmful desires
and practice moderation in all things. Amen

Good Directions

The great thing in this world is not so much where we stand,
as in what direction we are moving.
Oliver Wendell Holmes

When we're driving in an unfamiliar city, we're apt to miss a turn off or start heading down the wrong street. In short, we get lost! So we stop and either look at our map or ask someone for help in getting back where we're supposed to be.

Our journey through life takes us all through unfamiliar territory. Not one person among us can say we've been at this place and at this time, so if we lose our bearings from time to time, it's hardly a big surprise. And God isn't surprised, either. Instead, He does what only He can do. He guides us to the right path, shows us how to get back on it, and reminds us that He—and no one else—has been this way before.

If you're feeling as if you're traveling down the wrong road right now, stop and consult the one who truly knows the whole route.

Lead me back, dear God, to the right path. Amen

Free to Good Home

A good laugh is sunshine in a house.
William Makepeace Thackeray

What are your pet peeves? Those are the everyday annoyances that are like a swarm of gnats—you just can't seem to get away from them.

While pet peeves consist of minor, inconsequential aspects of modern life, they can affect your attitude in a big way. A pet peeve once adopted triggers irritation, even anger, every time you come across it. It has the power to turn your day from good to bad, your mood from sweet to sour, your thoughts from positive to negative. Every pet peeve you allow into your life sets your attention on the irritations instead of the blessings all around you.

To handle pet peeves and all the small frustrations of life, God has given you a handy response—humor. If you can't change it (robocalls aren't going away any time soon), laugh at it. And when one starts buzzing around your head, swat it!

Lift me with laughter, dear God,
when life's irritations are getting me down. Amen

In the Right Place

When I am weak, then am I strong.
2 Corinthians 12:10

Hardly anyone would choose weakness over strength, or helplessness over power. In our world, strength and power earn us perks, including the admiration of others (and often a big ego, too). In God's world, however, weakness and helplessness are essential to spiritual growth and maturity. They are what bring the greatest rewards.

When you admit your weaknesses, you grasp the impossibility of following God's path with anything approaching perfection. When you find yourself helpless in matters of the spirit, you possess a clear picture of the human condition. That's how both weakness and helplessness work to deepen your understanding of life's realities...to give you the ability to feel empathy and compassion...and to awaken in you a need for God.

Feeling weak? Can't deny you're helpless? That's quite all right. You're in exactly the right place for God to give you true strength and genuine power—the kind that no one can take away.

Dear God, grant me Your strength in place of my weaknesses.
Amen

Do Pray the Small Stuff

Nothing is too small a subject for prayer,
because nothing is too small to be the subject of God's care.
Henry Thomas Hamblin

Have you ever decided not to pray about something? Your reasoning might have sounded something like this: "What's bothering me is such small potatoes that I'm embarrassed to take it to God. After all, there are people with much, much bigger problems than mine, and I feel totally ungrateful whining about...." You finish the sentence!

Okay, so what you have on your mind is nothing compared to the hardships others are facing right now, but God still wants to hear from you. Big or small, your concerns matter to Him. Anything affecting your spiritual health, growth, and serenity matters to Him. Whatever keeps you from living life to the fullest and finding joy in the blessings around you is something you can bring to Him in prayer.

Small stuff, big stuff—it's all the stuff of prayer when you know God as your heavenly Father who cares about you. He will listen, and He will answer according to what He knows is best for you. Do pray the small stuff!

Heavenly Father, thank You for listening to
even the smallest of my concerns. Amen

A Way of Looking

Joy can be real only if people look upon their life as a service,
and have a definite object in life outside themselves
and their personal happiness.
Leo Tolstoy

"Look out for number one" is the mantra of many who would reach ambitious goals and achieve personal satisfaction. Certainly we're responsible for our own health, safety, and wellbeing, but we push the mantra aside when we start thinking about what makes a personally satisfying and spiritually rewarding life. For this we might say instead, "look out for everyone else."

Your wishes and desires count, of course. They come between you and genuine joy, however, if they count all the time... every time...24/7...regardless of how they affect others. Your preferences hinder true happiness if they're your number one focus and you only rarely, or never, put them aside to give your time and attention to someone else's feelings and needs.

Looking out for others means simply this: Support their good plans and ideas. Encourage them with kindly words and share with them a portion of the resources God has given to you. Then you will know God's number one blessing: true, heart-deep fulfillment.

Dear God, help me be more attentive
to the needs and desires of others. Amen

What Never Changes

Today is not yesterday: we ourselves change; how can our works and thoughts, if they are always to be the fittest, continue always the same? Change, indeed is painful, yet ever needful.
Thomas Carlyle

Say you arrive at your favorite park, picnic basket in hand, and suddenly the wind picks up, the sky darkens, and the clouds let loose with a torrent of rain. With barely a moment's notice, your plans are changed, at least for this afternoon.

From time to time, a storm passes through our lives that changes everything—everything we've planned, prepared for, and ever imagined would happen. These events may have developed over time or advanced quickly, but there came the day when we found ourselves face to face with a whole new reality. That's when we realized that our old plans were as unworkable as an outdoor picnic on a rainy day.

God's plans, however, remain constant, even in stormy weather. Though something may change everything else, His love, compassion, and purpose for you still stand. No rainstorms brought on by outside circumstances or troubles stemming from personal missteps can alter the warmth and sunshine of God's good feelings toward you.

Assure me, dear God, that You are still at my side
when the storms of life threaten to get me down. Amen

God's Good Will

Faith consists, not in ignorance, but in knowledge,
and that, not only of God, but also of the divine will.
John Calvin

It's one thing to acknowledge that God is God and to thank Him for the blessings in your life...praise Him for creating a world of beauty and splendor...talk to Him about your needs and wishes. But it's quite another thing to accept His divine will in all matters concerning you, including the desires you hold closest to your heart.

From our point of view, the will of God can be mysterious, perplexing, and even mind-boggling at times. Then again, God's will can open marvelous opportunities, introduce us to facets of the human soul we never would have imagined existed, and enable us to spend our time and talents in positive, life-affirming ways.

God's will is active, purposeful, and at all times wise. You waste time and energy trying to fight it, because after all, God is God! The best way to fulfill His will for you is to accept it—embrace it!—and discover all He has in mind for your ultimate good.

Strengthen my faith in You, dear God,
and help me discern Your divine will in all things. Amen

A Matter of Motivation

*The very best and utmost attainment in this life
is to remain still and let God act and speak in thee.*
Meister Eckhart

Picture two women, both faithful volunteers in a local
soup kitchen. No matter the foul weather, what else is
going on in their lives, or how they wake up feeling, you
can depend on them to arrive at the kitchen and prepare
meals for the needy with efficiency and enthusiasm.
But there's an important difference between the two,
and that's their reason for being there. The first woman
wants to hear God praise her for giving. The second,
deeply grateful for all God has given her, desires to give
back.

As long as your focus remains on yourself—even
when you are extending kindness, compassion, and help
to others—you can't experience the joy of God working through you. Instead, look to His compassion for
you. Remember His great kindness to you. Receive His
forgiveness, comfort, and peace. Motivated by a heart
overflowing with thankfulness, go and serve.

Let His Spirit work in you as you, spurred by gratitude, give back to others.

**Dear God, in response to Your love for me,
let me share Your love with others. Amen**

Fess Up, Start Over

*If you board the wrong train, it is no use
running along the corridor in the other direction.*
Dietrich Bonhoeffer

We've heard the jokes about male drivers who refuse to admit they're lost, even though they're heading in the wrong direction. In life's journey, however, most of us fess up when we're wrong and make a U-turn, except when it comes to certain decisions we've made.

If we start on a path with great enthusiasm, even boasting about our great destiny, it's humiliating to find ourselves on a dead end street. Indeed, the pain of embarrassment can keep us continuing on the road we chose, even though we realize it's the wrong one. Not admitting we're wrong becomes more important than fessing up, turning around, and getting back in the direction we want to go.

If you think you're headed in the wrong direction, it's no shame to admit it. You're not the same person you were when you started out, and you've discovered this isn't the road for you. There's nothing better to do but fess up, turn around, and start over!

**Dear God, enable me to find new paths,
paths in sync with your will for my life. Amen**

Talk or Act?

*We have too many high-sounding words
and too few actions that correspond with them.*
Abigail Adams

People who promise the most aren't always the ones who do the most. Perhaps that's because they're so busy declaring what they will do that they leave themselves no time to actually do it! In any group we're in, we soon learn who are the talkers and who are the doers.

It's easy to over-promise. We want to be there for our loved ones. We aspire to generously support causes and organizations we care about. We wish we could single-handedly fix what's wrong and lift every burden. But God has given no one that kind of power. Instead, what He has given is this: The ability to do one small thing to ease life for someone else. The resources to share a portion of what we have with those in need. The time to say a kindly word and offer practical help to someone right next to us.

Those sound like small things, but they make more of a difference than a stream of high-sounding, but unfulfilled, words.

**Dear God, grant that I will always
back up my words with work. Amen**

Your Cheering Section

When you get into a tight place and everything goes against you,
till it seems as though you could not hold on a minute longer,
never give up then, for that is just the place
and time when the tide will turn.
Harriet Beecher Stowe

If you have ever played team sports, you've felt the energy, affirmation, and positive vibes of a cheering crowd. If you have ever performed on stage, you've experienced the warmth, acceptance, and admiration of an appreciative audience.

Yet you don't have to hit the arena or stand up on stage to know what a difference encouragement makes! Perhaps you remember when a little praise—even if it was simply "Good job!"—made the difference between giving up and continuing on. Just knowing that someone's out there rooting for you goes a long way to keep you moving until you reach your goal.

Who's in your cheering section? Some you can name, but others are friends, coworkers, acquaintances, and even strangers who have admired what you're doing and silently send a thumbs-up your way. Keep going, because encouragement is all around you—and don't forget to include God, your number-one encourager for all time!

Thank You, dear God, for cheering me on,
especially when I want to quit. Amen

Angels Around You

He shall give his angels charge over thee,
to keep thee in all thy ways.
Psalm 91:11

Angels in artwork are often depicted as hovering creatures with flowing robes and sweeping wings. They appear sweet and gentle, but we come away with a narrow and sentimental idea of the magnificent heavenly beings God created.

Far from fragile, angels go wherever God sends them—and that may be anywhere a person suffers, grieves, cries out for help, or faces danger. They're strong enough to help and protect the weakest among us, most especially children. With God's compassion in their hearts, they befriend the lonely and ease the sick. With God's messages on their lips, they deliver His wisdom and warnings, His directions and promises to human hearts.

Angels are part of your life—never doubt it. All around you there are countless angels you can't see, as well as those you can see in the faces of family members, friends, and neighbors. Angels are all those who reach out to you with acts of heavenly kindness and love.

Thank You, dear God, for all the angels
who guide, protect, and care for me. Amen

Good Anger

We praise a man who is angry on the right grounds,
against the right persons, in the right manner,
at the right moment, and for the right length of time.
Aristotle

Anger has gotten a bad rap! Often people believe that anger is never God's will, and they feel guilty when they give in to it. While out-of-control anger is harmful, pointless, and not God's desire, good anger is a godly response to ungodly situations.

Your good anger motivates you to take practical and productive steps to change wrongs to rights and turn cruelty to kindness. Good anger calls the guilty to account, but ends as soon as restitution has been made and the matter is settled. It thinks before it speaks, never lashing out in the heat of the moment. It accuses, but accuses rightly and without malice. It shouts until it's heard where injustice exists, but quiets after a fair solution has been reached.

Anger is like a tool on a workbench. Use it carelessly, and you endanger yourself and everyone around you. But use anger the way God intends for you to use it, and it's a powerful instrument for change, compassion, renewal, and restoration.

Dear God, help me use my anger in ways that work
for the common good and are pleasing to You. Amen

A Positive Story

How can we send the highest love to another
if we do not have it for ourselves?
Prentice Mulford

"I'm such a klutz!" "That was so dumb of me!" Have you heard yourself use similar words? Do those phrases sound like what goes through your mind as you look back on your day? If so, it's time to rewrite the script!

Very often we talk to and about ourselves in terms we'd never use to describe someone else. While we'll give others the benefit of a doubt, we hold ourselves and our behavior up to a harsh, unforgiving light. Consequently, we develop a negative self-image. We believe the bad spin we're putting on everything we do.

God's love for you invites you—urges you!—to love yourself. Every day, affirm your God-given identity as a child of the heavenly Father. No one, not even you, has permission to put you down. Challenge, freshen, and brighten the things you say to yourself and the words you use around others. Think and speak from a loving heart. Tell your story with compassion, understanding, humor, and most of all, joy.

Dear God, grant me a healthy and wholesome love for myself
so that I may love others. Amen

An Individual Decision

Do not wish to be anything but what you are.
Francis de Sales

God has made each of us unique, right down to the swirls at the tips of our fingers! Who (except God) would have thought to do that? Yet many of us spend a lifetime trying to look, talk, and act like everyone else.

Though God has molded us, shaped us, and even tinted us differently, we admire only one standard of beauty. Where He has given us diverse talents, skills, and abilities, we strive for some and ignore others. What God calls distinctive, we declare flawed. Not only do these judgments erode our sense of self-worth, they also blind us to the God-given value of others.

God invites you to see yourself—and everyone around you—as He sees you. And what does He see? God sees an individual He has put in the world for a reason. He has given you the appearance, talents, and abilities you need to fulfill His purpose for you. Why would you want to be any different than just the way you are?

Dear God, help me see myself with Your eyes
of love and acceptance. Amen

What Humility Looks Like

Humility must always be doing its work
like a bee making its honey in the hive.
Theresa of Avila

She likes it when others notice her particularly becoming outfit, her new hair style, her engaging smile. When others compliment her, she feels warm inside, and she's drawn to those who make her feel appreciated and loved. Is she a humble person?

Not if she lets the accolades fill her head instead of soften her heart. If she takes the admiration of others as her due, she harbors an elevated sense of her own importance. If she finds it impossible to like someone who doesn't pay special attention to her, she definitely isn't humble.

She is certainly humble, however, if she sees herself in the light of God's love. Because of His many blessings to her, she's able to contribute to the wellbeing of others. Yes, she receives praise, but she gives it, too. Sure she likes attention, but if she doesn't get it, she isn't disturbed. She's pleased simply being who she is and privileged to be whose she is.

Humility not only looks good, but it feels good, too.

Grant me, dear God, the blessing of genuine humility
as I serve You and others with my life. Amen

God Restores Hope

Despondency is ingratitude; hope is God's worship.
Henry Ward Beecher

In times of loss, all our thoughts turn to what's missing—spouse, family member, or friend. Perhaps there's the loss of health or mobility, home or livelihood. If we let it, any one of these life-altering events could leave us not temporarily grieving, but permanently bemoaning our unfortunate and painful circumstances.

God restores hope where loss has left a gaping chasm. As if lifting you in His wings, He makes it possible for you to look toward tomorrow in confidence that there will be better days ahead. No, it won't be the future you thought would unfold for you, but a future still under God's command and within His good plans for you.

Turn your thoughts from loss to hope. Open the eyes of your soul and see His presence filling the empty space that's in your life right now. Rest at ease in Him, relying on Him to show you the way ahead. It might not be easy at first, but where there's faith, there's always hope.

In times of loss, dear God, fill my heart with hope
in Your continuing love and care for me. Amen

A Good Fit

Old things are passed away;
behold, all things are become new.
2 Corinthians 5:17

When you follow God, you won't always fit right in. Sometimes you'll find yourself among people who are using words you don't feel comfortable hearing, much less saying. There might be places you go that you realize aren't the places God would have you visit.

What might have fit you before doesn't now because you've gone forward in your spiritual life, and you continue to make good progress. More and more, you're discovering how much higher God's standards are than those of many people around you. As you let God shape your heart and mind, you start making God-informed decisions and relying on God-spoken truths. No wonder there are times and places you don't fit in!

Be encouraged, because not fitting in is a sign of God's Spirit at work in you, forming you into a spiritually taller, healthier, and more robust person. As you obey Him, you'll be surprised how many others may "see fit" to follow you!

Dear God, please continue to shape my heart and mind according to Your thoughts, not mine. Amen

Tech Savvy

Wishing to be friends is quick work,
but friendship is a slow ripening fruit.
Aristotle

Social media have linked us in ways not possible only a few decades ago. We're able to keep in touch with people across the country and around the world with ease. We can talk with them and read about their daily lives in real time. Thanks to technology, we can share thoughts, feelings, experiences, and perspectives instantly!

Because you're able to share in the daily joys and sorrows, celebrations and challenges of your faraway friends, you have a responsibility. God's Spirit prompts you to respond to them from the heart, uplift and encourage them with expressions of hope, and pray for their needs. Your meaningful and timely words today can assure your friends of God's love and compassion for all people.

Technology enables you to expand your understanding, increase your knowledge, and bless others every day. Used for God's good purposes, technology links people across the miles, heart to heart.

Show me, dear God, how I can use all the means
available to me to bless my many friends. Amen

Take the Pressure Off

Anxiety is a word of unbelief or unreasoning dread.
We have no right to allow it. Full faith in God puts it to rest.
Horace Bushnell

When we're under intense pressure, we're more likely than ever to lose things—an even temper, positive attitude, good judgment, and sense of fairness. Unbearable stress pushes us to blame others for their seeming indifference to our predicament, and tension makes clear thinking next to impossible.

In all likelihood, you know how it is to feel this way. Because you're a responsible person, you take your responsibilities seriously. People depend on you, and you have no intention of letting them down. There's stress! There's tension! But there are times when there's nothing you can do except step back, let go, and let God take the pressure off.

Close your eyes for a few moments. Picture yourself giving to Him everything causing you intense pressure. All those to-do's you're facing? All the needs you have to take care of? Hand them all over to Him until there's nothing left. Be still in His soothing presence. Lose yourself in His abundant peace.

Dear God, lift anxiety from me
and enable me to find rest in Your peace. Amen

A Vital Voice

Oftentimes nothing profits more than self-esteem,
grounded on what is just and right and well-managed.
John Milton

At times you hesitate to speak up. You hear what others are saying, and you don't feel comfortable telling them that you have a different opinion or challenging their assumptions. It's understandable, because you want to respect and support others.

Yet speaking up could be exactly what God is calling you to do. When what others are saying threatens your wellbeing, peace of mind, safety, security, or plans and desires, you have a God-given right to say so. The anger or disapproval of others is a small price to pay if what you say prevents them from taking advantage of your goodwill or acting in ways that harm you. When your cause is just, your voice is vital.

Pray for God to give you the strength and confidence you need to speak up for yourself when the occasion demands. Your voice may be exactly what God will use to provide for your needs and to send you the opportunities He has in mind for you.

Strengthen me, dear God, to speak up
for my just and rightful needs. Amen

Big Gains

Take delight in the LORD,
and he will give you the desires of your heart.
Psalm 37:4 NIV

Your perspective shifts when God comes first in your life. Personal preferences give way to God's commandments, and self-centeredness morphs into God-centeredness. Your focus moves from your will to God's will, from your reasoning to His wisdom.

Does this sound like giving up who you are, what you want, and what excites and interests you? It is sometimes, but here's what you get in return: a heart filled with love for others...a mind set on productive, worthwhile aims and activities...an outlook of optimism and trust in the future. You receive resilience to carry you through life's troubles...trust in your ability to thrive, no matter what the circumstances...faith to lean on in times of loss...joy to glow in your life and light the way for others. God gives you the ability to take immense delight in all the blessings He showers on you.

Yes, you might give up something when you place God first in your life. But you gain the desires of your heart.

Dear God, enable me to give up what's not pleasing to You. Bless me, and dwell in the center of my heart. Amen

God's Sign

*It is no use walking anywhere to preach
unless our walking is our preaching.*
Francis of Assisi

During Jesus' earthly ministry, many people asked Him for a sign. They wanted to see Him work a miracle before they would believe His words of compassion, forgiveness, and love. Today, things haven't changed. There are still people requiring a sign, demanding a miracle, asking God for proof before they'll put their trust in Him.

God's answer hasn't changed, either. Proof of His existence lies in the minute complexity and marvelous design of the universe, of each person, and of you. Proof of His power resides in every heart that has been dramatically transformed by His life-affirming, life-giving message of forgiveness and redemption. Proof of His ongoing work among people comes seldom in supernatural signs, but daily in the goodness, kindness, gentleness, and God-filled joy of people. People like you.

You may have never thought of it this way before, but it's true: When you apply God's rules and His wisdom to your life, you are one of His signs!

**Dear God, grant me the privilege of living
as a sign to others of Your love. Amen**

Less Is More

*The only simplicity that matters
is the simplicity of the heart.*
G. K. Chesterton

A simple life! Though it doesn't require us to take up residence in a bare room on an isolated mountaintop, it does mean getting rid of clutter right where we are—all that stuff we tend to accumulate but never really use or enjoy. Clutter includes high-cost services we can barely afford and high-maintenance products we have little time to maintain. Wouldn't life be simpler without them?

A truly simple life, however, means more than cleaning out your closets or reducing your phone bill. It calls for a change of attitude from getting to giving...from desire to contentment...from constant entertainment to inner quiet, joy, and peace. Just as excessive possessions weigh you down with stress and obligations, so do uncontrolled emotions and yearnings.

If you'd like simpler, calmer, and more manageable days, think of what you can do without, both materially and emotionally. You'll be surprised how much more enjoyable life will become and how much lighter you'll feel.

**Dear God, show me where I can simplify my way of living
so that I may live more fully in You. Amen**

Coping with Pain

With the help of the thorn in my foot,
I spring higher than anyone with sound feet.
Søren Kierkegaard

How do you handle physical pain? If "not well!" is your answer, join the crowd! Few would willingly take on pain, but there come times when we have no choice—the root canal must be performed. Open-heart surgery is necessary. The baby is about to be born. Pain is part of life, and it's unavoidable.

What you can avoid, however, is letting physical pain rule, and ruin, your life. Fearing you might feel pain causes you emotional suffering before the body has experienced so much as a twinge. Dwelling on your present hurts intensifies pain, making it harder for you to find relief. It's painful! But you can learn to cope with actual pain and minimize its debilitating effect.

Ask for help. Others have been where you are, and they can give you practical advice. Relying on God's healing power, you can learn to set your mind on changing what's changeable and accepting what can't be changed. There's a way to handle pain productively and rediscover joy in living and in life.

Help me, dear God, overcome my fear of pain
and handle the pain I have. Amen

Good Courage

Be strong and of a good courage.
Joshua 1:9

The firefighter who rushes into a burning home, the rescuer who climbs a rocky mountain cliff, the lifeguard who dives into a roiling sea...those people have courage! Repeatedly we read of men and women who, for the sake of saving another person, perform breathtaking acts of courage.

Yet everyday acts of courage often go unnoticed. There's the woman who, despite a devastating divorce, pulls herself together so she can be there for her children. There's the man who overcomes a debilitating addiction by refusing to give up on himself, although others did. There's the child who won't believe she can't, because she knows she can. And there are people like you...people who take the ups and downs of life with resolve, patience, and good humor...who persevere and triumph...who take on their responsibilities, no matter how heavy, with humility and grace.

God helps and He blesses people of good courage... people exactly like you.

Strengthen me, dear God, and bless me with the faith
and fortitude it takes to live courageously. Amen

A Recipe for Success

God gives us always strength enough, and sense enough,
for everything He wants us to do.
John Ruskin

You pull out a recipe, ingredients, measuring cups, bowls, and a cookie sheet, and you're all set to mix up a batch of your favorite cookies. You have no doubt that you can do it, because you have everything you need right at your fingertips.

You have everything you need to love and serve others, too. God has given you the ingredients—a desire to bless others in meaningful ways and daily opportunities to do so. He has filled your heart with generous measures of thoughtfulness, compassion, and kindness, and He keeps refilling so you'll never run out. With listening ears, caring words, and helping hands, you're all set to start mixing up a batch of God-sent blessings.

Oh, about the recipe? He's supplied that, too. The guidance and encouragement, counsel and wisdom found in Scripture is God's complete recipe for using what He has given you to love and serve others. Follow His instructions, and savor the sweetness of life!

Dear God, thank You for giving me
everything I need to love and serve others. Amen

Interdependence

*Even in the common affairs of life, in love,
friendship, and marriage, how little security have we
when we trust our happiness in the hands of others.*
William Hazlitt

Ensconced in our comfort zone, we shy away from challenging ourselves to try new things or branching out to discover all we're really capable of doing. We become so dependent on another person or our circumstances that we doubt our ability to succeed on our own. Or perhaps there's someone who's inappropriately dependent on us...someone whose self-worth is at a low ebb because we're taking care of everything.

Complete independence, however, isn't the answer. Without meaningful relationships, life would lose its luster. Increasingly, we'd find ourselves unable and unwilling to trust others, to accept their love and encouragement, and to give of ourselves for the good of someone else.

Balanced, healthy relationships not only allow you to flourish, but others to flourish, as well. Interdependence—a bond of mutual care and concern, cooperation and support—allows everyone to grow together. Joyful interdependence is God's way of connecting you with those closest to you so each person gives and receives, sacrifices and benefits, loves and is loved in return.

**Dear God, help me maintain healthy and balanced relationships
so all of us may reach our full potential. Amen**

Get Noticed

God loves each of us as if there were only one of us.
Augustine

In a busy family...a competitive workplace...a bustling community, loneliness can shadow our days. Though surrounded by people, we feel no one notices our contributions or cares about our thoughts and needs.

How easily loneliness turns to bitterness! Resentment darkens our attitude to the point we want to lash out at our situation and those around us. But this isn't a productive response, and we know it. What we desperately need is assurance that we're noticed, loved, and cherished, and only God can fully meet our deepest of needs.

If you feel lonely right now, remember God's lasting love for you as an individual. No matter what the people around you may say or do, God holds you in His sight, in His hands, and in His heart. And once you realize how much you're worth in His sight, you can't help but walk a little taller...speak up a little more often... become a little more visible...get noticed for the God-cherished person you are.

Thank You, dear God, for Your continuing love for me no matter how others may see me or think of me. Amen

Families Like Ours

If God can work through me,
He can work through anyone.
Francis of Assisi

Families in the Bible act a lot like families today. While there are numerous illustrations of tender love and mutual devotion, there are also examples of families torn apart by intense jealousy, blatant infidelity, sibling rivalry, and rebellious teens. Even in the most conflict-ridden families, however, God works through husbands and wives, sons and daughters, cousins and in-laws, uncles and aunts.

Nothing has changed. In the middle of family disputes and dissension, God turns helplessness to competence and heartbreak to hope, just as He did back in Bible times. Then as now, struggle can drive us to fervent prayer, where we learn to put more reliance than ever on Him. Our bond with Him strengthens, and our relationships with family members deepen as we work with them to resolve our mutual problems.

Family conflicts test our commitment and our faith. Our struggles put our values and our loyalties on the line. They can bring out the worst, or the very best, in each of us.

In times of conflict, dear God, grant me
the light and wisdom of Your guidance. Amen

Absolutely True

Truth is the exact opposite of the evidence of the senses.
It ever declares the perfection of God and all His works.
Henry Thomas Hamblin

What if you went out one day and discovered that all street signs and landmarks had been moved to random locations throughout the city? Imagine if this happened frequently and completely without warning. Someone's playing with your mind, right?

By declaring that there's no such thing as absolute truth, someone is definitely playing with your mind—and your faith. Believe the claim, and you're traveling through life without reliable street signs, because no one has the authority to say "right road" or "wrong road." You have no landmarks to go by, because they've all been taken away, or moved, or declared a delusion. Nothing's absolute.

One of God's great gifts to you is proclamation of the truth—a truth that doesn't change with the times or is dependent on human opinion or agreement. Every day you have His eternal promises to point you in the right direction and His fixed rules to go by. When God speaks, it's the truth—absolutely.

Dear God, please put Your truth at the center
of my heart, mind, and soul. Amen

Serenity Today

Seek not that the things which happen should happen as you wish;
but wish the things which happen to be as they are,
and you will have a tranquil flow of life.
Epictetus

"What are you trying to do?" And she'll tell you: "Make my mother-in-law stop criticizing me." "Get my son to bring the grandkids over more often." "Make sure a snowstorm won't interfere with our holiday plans." But try as she might, she has no control over her mother-in-law's attitude, her son's decisions, or the weather tomorrow.

But she does have control over what she spends her time trying to accomplish. She can set her mind on changing people's traits and fretting over events outside herself, or she can choose to put her efforts toward acceptance, tolerance, and understanding. She can decide to fix everything and everyone who crosses her path, or she can do a few fixes on her attitude and perspective. She can fight it, or turn away and let it go.

Serenity isn't what will miraculously descend on you if you could get everything to meet your preferences and expectations. Rather, serenity is what will naturally come to you as soon as, despite your circumstances, you choose it.

Dear God, help me let go of useless anxiety
and choose the blessing of serenity. Amen

Trust Him on That

I think we may safely trust a good deal more than we do.
Henry David Thoreau

Few of us can say that no one has ever disappointed us. In a relatively minor matter or in one of utmost importance, we placed our trust in someone who proved unworthy of it. Hurt, some of us decide not to trust anyone again; others among us continue to trust, but with caution and care. Before giving our trust, we ask ourselves, "Is this person trustworthy?"

Family ties, friendships, working relationships, and community togetherness are positive and productive only when we're willing to trust one another. Even though someone may let us down from time to time, or we'll mistakenly place our trust in the wrong person, we cannot live a fulfilling and joyous life without trust. In addition, our own self-respect and reputation among people depend on our being worthy of the trust others place in us.

God, who is completely trustworthy, invites you to put your trust in Him. Trust His care and compassion for you. Trust His understanding. Most of all, trust His love—it will never disappoint.

Dear God, help me place my trust fully in You. Amen

Bit by Bit

We must follow, not force providence.
William Shakespeare

Sometimes God reveals His presence through a huge, life-altering event. For example, a near-death experience or sudden revelation has turned certain individuals into committed, passionate followers of Jesus. More often than not, however, God works bit by bit, year by year, in the lives of His people.

Each day that you open your heart to His promptings, you advance in spiritual awareness. All the little acts of kindness you do because you want to follow in His way reflect His presence in your life. Your growth in godliness happens slowly, sometimes without you even realizing that you're making progress. But you are, and as His work in you continues, you move forward one step at a time.

God will reveal His presence to you, but how He does it and how quickly He does it is His choice alone. Rest at ease, knowing that your spiritual health and wellbeing is His specialty. Let Him take care of it His way.

Make Your presence known to me, dear God,
in the way You know is best for me. Amen

A Note of Gratitude

In every thing give thanks.
1 Thessalonians 5:18

Gratitude has been called the root of all other virtues, and it's easy to understand why. When your heart is filled with gratitude, you're focused on blessings. Focusing on blessings makes you feel good inside, gives you an optimistic outlook, and provides you with hope for the future. With such a positive attitude, you make good things happen, more blessings follow—and more gratitude grows!

As you can see, genuine gratitude is more than a begrudging admission that you don't have it as bad as some other people. Being truly thankful isn't a trick designed to shake you out of the doldrums. Rather, it's a God-sown seed in your heart that flowers each time you turn to Him in praise for the privilege of belonging to Him. What better blessing can you imagine?

Let God's Spirit plant the seed of genuine gratitude in your heart. It will make a difference, not just for today, but for every day of a fruitful, joy-full life.

Dear God, thank You for everything,
especially for the privilege of knowing You! Amen

A Better Response

Life appears to me too short to be spent
in nursing animosity or registering wrongs.
Charlotte Brontë

There's something about rage and bitterness. They're dramatic, and at times we believe they're justified. Certainly we're enraged when life turns our good plans inside out. Naturally we're bitter when someone takes away love, support, or provision we had every reason to depend on. But rage and bitterness make a bad situation worse.

Rage and bitterness increase to the point that the white glare of our imagination blinds us to reason. All we can focus on is what happened to us, what happened to them! Even if we're the victim of obvious injustice, untamed wrath blinds us to how God can work to help us and others in our same predicament.

When social injustices affect you, those you care about, or people in your heart, respond with God-given wisdom. Let Him inform your actions. Let Him open your eyes so you can see how to help in real and practical ways. Rage and bitterness are natural reactions, but a thoughtful, active, and effective response is better.

Guard my heart, dear God, against anger and bitterness. Amen

Get Serious

If you do not hear reason, she will rap you on the knuckles.
Benjamin Franklin

Most pastors have heard someone say, "I'll get serious about God as soon as I get my life back in order." And most would reply: "Get serious about God, and your life will get back in order."

Indeed, it's life without God that sends the threads of life flying in every direction. Without God, we lose our direction and our real purpose. We're not sure what we believe or why we believe it. More and more, we rely on our own thinking, our own abilities, our own drive, and our own resources. What happens, then, when something goes awry? We've got problems—big problems.

You might have problems in your life, but you have one huge problem if you try to solve them without God. He's there to clean up messes, offer solutions, and help you get your life back in order. If you hear anyone say she's trying to do it on her own, tell her this: Get serious about God now, and the messes in your life will take care of themselves.

Open Your arms to me, dear God,
in the middle of my messes. Amen

The Voice of Experience

*Life affords no higher pleasure
than that of surmounting difficulties.
Samuel Johnson*

The person you know who's "been there, done that"
is the one you want to talk to. No matter how much
information you can look up online or get from other
sources, you probably will give special credence to the
voice of experience.

What's true about exploring a career, deciding on a
neighborhood, or thinking about a vacation spot is also
true when calamity strikes. Who better than someone
who's come through a similar catastrophe to help us
face our new reality? Who else can say "I understand"
and mean it than the person who is successfully coping
with the same affliction?

Those who have gone before us through their own
darkness shine a light for all who follow. Their inner
strength inspires us, and they walk as a model to show
us how God never takes away without giving something
in return. They know it's true, because they've "been
there, done that."

**In dark paths, dear God, please put people in my life
who can light the way through
and help me successfully cope. Amen**

A Great Solution

When a person is down in the world,
an ounce of help is better than a pound of preaching.
Edward Bulwer-Lytton

A friend confides a difficulty she's having with her grown son. A family member comes with a long list of problems and complaints. A coworker tells you he can't get along with the people on his team. As you listen, solutions run through your mind. You know how you'd handle it if you were in their shoes, and so you...

Tell them? But often the best help you can give is your willingness to listen. As your friend, family member, or coworker talks to you, they're also talking to themselves. Their thoughts may have swirled around their minds like a kite in a gale, but in expressing them out loud, things become clearer. They start talking about their solutions, ones that might work for the person actually in their shoes—themselves.

And hear this: Don't be surprised if they go around telling everyone else what a great problem solver you are and how really, really smart you are! It happens to all good listeners.

Teach me to listen to others, dear God,
with the same compassion You listen to me. Amen

Perfectly Shaped

We are the clay, and thou our potter;
and we all are the work of thy hand.
Isaiah 64:8

God never wastes resources, and He uses every opportunity He sends your way. Interested in your spiritual growth and personal development, He takes who you are and where you are to form you into the person He wants you to become.

Look back through the years. Thank Him for your blessings, of course. But also thank Him for the challenges and misfortunes you have confronted, because they have formed the foundation of your present-day wisdom, knowledge, and experience. Thank Him as you think about the countless "coincidences" that have brought exciting, life-changing opportunities and have brought you into contact with the people who mean so much today. Praise Him with joyful thanksgiving as you look forward to a future filled with God-sent occasions to learn, laugh, and love.

Nothing you've experienced, whether good or bad, has been without a purpose. All the things you've been through are exactly the material God has used, and is still using, to shape you, to grow you, into His beloved, one-of-a-kind you.

Dear God, take me as I am and mold me
into the person you know I can be. Amen

Important Thoughts

The happiness of your life depends upon
the quality of your thoughts.
Marcus Aurelius

What's on your mind? Name one, two, or three topics that have been occupying your thoughts lately, and you'll know exactly what's most important to you right now. You'll have a clear picture of where you're investing your time and concentration. Do you like what you see?

So often we go about our days doing one thing, but thinking about something entirely different. Fear of the future, for example, shadows the sunshine today. Anxiety about money, health, or relationships saps the joy God intends us to find in the world around us. More important than all that's actually going on outside is what's going on inside our minds!

Let God take first place in your thoughts today. Talk to Him about those other important topics that have held your mind captive for so long, and ask Him to help you put them in perspective. They're important, yes, but not more important than your God.

Dear God, let my thoughts focus on You
so I may know Your peace. Amen

On a Quiet Day

*Prayers should be the key of the day
and the lock of the night.*
Proverb

In case of emergency, call 911...sound the alarm...use the fire extinguisher...put on a life vest...say a prayer. But of all things specific to urgent situations only, prayer isn't one of them. Prayer belongs in all situations. You can use it in all cases, even in the most boring, humdrum, routine day you could imagine.

God desires a lively, vibrant relationship with you, and that's why He invites you to meet with Him in prayer regularly and frequently. As you reserve time for Him alone, your awareness of His presence increases. You become more attuned to His voice in your heart and His work in your life. Your words to Him and your attentiveness to His response nurture the connection with Him that God has made possible for you to enjoy.

Why wait for an emergency to start your conversation with Him? On a normal, quiet, no-surprises day, a few minutes in His presence can be the beginning of a life-changing relationship!

**Thank You, dear God, for inviting me to pray every day,
even when nothing special is going on! Amen**

Forward in Forgiveness

How unhappy is he who cannot forgive himself.
Publilius Syrus

If you like to sew, you no doubt need to rip out stitches from time to time. You realize (too late!) that the seam you just finished sewing is crooked, or it puckers, or the thread knotted underneath. Before going on with the project, you sigh, pick out the stitches, and redo the seam.

Unfortunately, there's no chance to redo a carelessly spoken word, rash action, or embarrassing slip-up. While apologies, repentance, and reparations are necessary to relieve the sorrowful soul, there's no undoing what happened. Try as we might, what's been done can't be undone.

But here's what you *can* do. Strengthened by the certainty of God's forgiveness, you can find true peace of mind and heart. Wiser and more aware than before, you can understand and empathize with others who are struggling with self-reproach or lingering guilt. Relying on God to show you a better way, you can go forward with your head up and your heart happy.

Dear God, accept my sorrowing heart
and grant me Your forgiveness. Amen

Appreciate the Gift

Seek out that particular mental attribute
which makes you feel most deeply and vitally alive,
along with which comes the inner voice which says,
"This is the real me," and when
you have found that attitude, follow it.
William James

When you receive a marvelous gift, you don't put it on a shelf and never look at it again! Yet that's what happens whenever you hide the many wonderful talents and traits God has given to you.

Perhaps He has blessed you with a warm, outgoing personality and a natural love for people. Or maybe you have been blessed with a quiet and sensitive soul, quick to express compassion and let others know you care. Either way, it's possible that you hide a portion of your God-given individuality because you fear what others may say or think about you. But is that any way to treat a gift?

Imagine this: Your heavenly Father hands you several boxes, each containing a special trait, a unique characteristic, something He wants for you and you alone. So open the boxes one by one and lift out what's inside. Smile, thank God profusely, and then use it for the good of everyone around you. What a way to show Him your appreciation!

Dear God, I want to use the wonderful gifts
that You have so graciously given to me. Amen

It's Up to Him

He that shall humble himself shall be exalted.
Matthew 23:12

If you've ever stood at the foot of a majestic mountain or towering monument, you probably felt pretty small! Right in front of you loomed something that seemed so much greater, loftier, and more momentous than yourself.

Though God is more commanding than any mountain or monument, the comparison is one we can get our minds around. In front of Him, we stand small, weak, and insignificant. But unlike those imposing edifices, which never bend or even acknowledge our existence, God looks down to us. Even more, He comes down to us. He bends with outstretched arms to welcome us into His loving presence.

In front of God, human pride has no place. No matter what we do, we'll never come close to approaching His grand and glorious throne. How He must sigh when we frantically try to boost ourselves up. How He must smile when we allow Him to gently lift us.

Dear God, lift me up in Your arms of love and compassion so I may know the depth and breadth of Your love. Amen

Delight in the Day

All the great blessings of my life
are present in my thoughts today.
Phoebe Cary

When someone you love is tired and feeling down, you might urge rest and relaxation. You may even suggest that the two of you go out for an evening or a weekend away. Yes, you know how to encourage someone else to take time to relax, but how often do you encourage yourself to do the same thing?

Today, urge yourself to take a break. Do something not on your to-do list, but indulge in a whim or a walk in the sunshine. Sit by yourself and let your thoughts wander, or get a good book and let your imagination soar. Plan a day out doing something you love, or invite a friend to share an invigorating adventure with you. Do whatever you want to do—nix anything you *have* to do.

Treat yourself the way you treat the ones you love—encourage yourself to rest, rejuvenate, relax, and renew! They need to get away from time to time, and so do you.

Dear God, help me relax and delight
in the world You have made. Amen

Simply Peace

Let the past drift away with the water.
Proverb

How at peace with yourself are you today? Do old wounds weigh down your heart? Do regrets shadow your memories? If so, know this: You are not alone. Indeed, if you have never done anything that you've later lamented, it's doubtful that you've done much at all!

And know this, too. God is strong enough to lift the burden regret and sorrow cause. The light of His love and comfort scatters the shadow of uncertainty, and the gift of faith in His complete forgiveness lets joy, contentment, and peace flow back into your life. Why not give each nagging thought and niggling doubt to your heavenly Father? No matter where you are right now, you can do it. He is with you, ready to take each thing, one by one by one, from your shoulders.

Let Him refresh you. Breathe, walk, laugh, and love today with no apologies and no regrets. Simply peace.

Dear God, lift the burden of regret from my heart,
for I long for the peace You alone are able to give. Amen

Soul Food

In prayer one must hold fast and never let go,
because the one who gives up loses all.
Jane Frances de Chantal

Especially during our busy eat-and-run weeks, we're lucky to remember what we had for dinner the previous evening, much less what we ate last week. Yet the food has nourished us, given us the strength we needed to go about our daily lives, and contributed to our overall good health (unless, of course, one of those meals included a slice of fudge cheesecake!).

Whenever you take time out for reflection and prayer, you're receiving food for your soul. You might not be able to recall what it was you read or thought about yesterday, or even this morning, because not every spiritual mealtime is particularly memorable. Earth-shattering moments with God happen very rarely! Most of the time, it's a simple meal to keep you fed and nourished, strong and healthy in spirit. Trust Him to serve you everything you need, every day, when you come to Him.

Remembered or not, each moment with God nurtured your spirit, strengthened your faith, and has worked—and is still working—for your spiritual good.

Dear God, feed me with the sweetness of Your presence. Amen

Remembering When

Trouble creates a capacity to handle it.
Oliver Wendell Holmes

Perhaps you keep some photos of your cherished friends. Either stored online or pasted in a scrapbook, these pictures remind you of their smiles, their voices, and the fun times you've had together. Just looking at them makes you forget loneliness and brings on a warm, head-to-toe glow of happiness.

What you might not keep, however, is a mental "album" of times you've successfully solved a problem, overcome a challenge, and avoided a dangerous situation. Yet this kind of album is exactly what you need when you feel stymied—when you think you're beaten because you can't figure out what to do. In your imagination, look back through those pages! Time after time, you've won the day. Can you do it again? Of course you can!

In your prayers today, ask God to help you remember all the things you (and He) have come through. Never doubt that the two of you can do it again today and throughout all your tomorrows.

Thank You, dear God, for being with me in the past.
Let me depend on You today and forever! Amen

The Best Decisions

Choose always the way that seems the best,
however rough it may be.
Pythagoras

Most of us make decisions at precisely the wrong time. When we're down in the dumps, we're most apt to decide to give up. When major changes are taking place around us, we're almost compelled to make more changes, changes neither needed nor necessary at the time we opted to make them. It's no surprise, then, that our decisions under these circumstances aren't our better ones!

The best decision-making happens when you're feeling positive and upbeat. Especially when there's a significant choice in front of you, the more optimistic your outlook, the better your choice. Then if you elect to let go of a goal, it will be to choose another objective perhaps more worthwhile, challenging, and rewarding. If you decide to make a big change, it's because you believe it will enhance your life and the lives of others.

The best decisions come at the best of times! And at all times, let God guide your mind and heart as you make your life choices.

Dear God, help me make decisions from a positive point of view,
and guide me in all my choices. Amen

A Swimming Lesson

Keep the currents moving.
Don't let your life stagnate.
John Burroughs

If you have learned to swim, you probably know how to dog paddle. The dog paddle lets you bob in the water when you get tired of swimming, and to move short distances (preferably to the safety of the side of the pool!).

Though an excellent technique in the swimming pool, dog paddling gets us nowhere in life. The longer we're content to bob along wherever the current may take us, the less capable we feel in our ability to take big, bold strokes in a direction of our choosing. The more comfortable we get with the way things are, the less we'll find ourselves imagining the way things could be—and putting out an effort to make them happen.

Yes, there's a time to dog paddle when you need to catch your breath...look around...think...find a safe place to rest until you can figure out your next stroke. And then there's a time to dive in, explore the depths, and go the distance!

At the right time, dear God, grant me the courage
to dive in with confidence and enthusiasm. Amen

Sum of It All

*Inasmuch as ye have done it unto one of the least
of these my brethren, ye have done it unto me.*
Matthew 25:40

In the business of day-to-day living, it's easy to lose sight of life's purpose and meaning. We can't see how what we're doing from morning till night—the mundane chores, routine tasks, ordinary responsibilities—could possibly add up to something great, much less grand!

Yet each small undertaking done for others out of love for God brings His purpose for your life into reality. Though you don't count it as any big deal, your kind words cover wounded hearts with His comfort. Your thoughtful gestures lift sagging shoulders with His strength. Your everyday willingness to extend a welcome, dry a tear, share a burden, and make a difference for the better are all part of God's purpose for you.

All totaled, the things you do from day to day are the very things that give your life its grand, God-given meaning. Think about the hours ahead of you. What small thing could you say or do simply for the sake of blessing someone? You never know what it could end up amounting to!

**Dear God, never let me lose interest in doing
those things that really count with You. Amen**

The Heart of the Matter

Genius is the talent for seeing things straight.
It is seeing things in a straight line without any bend
or break or aberration of sight, seeing them as they are,
without any warping of vision.
Maude Adams

Perhaps you have been in a situation like this: People are seated around a table. Someone raises a thorny topic, and suddenly everyone starts shouting. As voices sharpen and tempers flare, the original topic explodes into dozens of topics. At last someone who has yet to say a word stands up and speaks. In a single sentence, she gets right to the heart of the matter. This, not all that, is what we should be discussing!

When you sit down to think through an upsetting issue in your life, watch out who else takes a chair—your inner voice. Her irrelevant distractions get you off-topic. Her spurious arguments jerk you in all directions. Her negative suggestions pull down your confidence, and her baseless misgivings create doubt, suspicion, and uncertainty. Suddenly you're dealing not with one issue, but dozens upon dozens of issues.

It's time to clear out the room and sit down with the only one who can get you back to the heart of the matter. Let God stand up and speak.

Speak, dear God, because I am listening. Amen

A Show of Strength

Nothing is so strong as gentleness;
nothing so gentle as real strength.
Francis de Sales

Who's the strongest one of all? According to many, the strongest is the person who possesses the most muscles, the greatest clout, the highest paycheck. But God, as He does so often, turns human reasoning on its head.

God-pleasing strength requires no show of toughness or display of might. It doesn't even call for money or status! Rather, His strength expresses itself in faith firmly rooted in His promises. The strength He offers gives you the spiritual muscle to resist failings that would take you away from His plan for your life. His strength provides to you the power to act with kindness, gentleness, patience, compassion, and love. Though these spiritual gifts are often scorned by the world as laughable weaknesses, they are great strengths in the eyes of God.

If your God-pleasing actions and good intentions have been mistaken for weaknesses, remember where real strength lies—in a heart brimming with evidence of God's Spirit at work in your life.

Dear God, grant me the kind of strength
that comes from faith in You. Amen

A View from the Mountaintop

If you wish to advance into the infinite,
explore the finite in all directions.
Johann von Goethe

Don't you love spiritual high points? You feel like you're standing at the crest of a mountain, in absolute unity with God and the universe! Then the next day comes, and you aren't as energetic, full of hope, or inspired as you were such a short time ago. From the mountaintop, you've landed flat on the plain.

Disappointed? Of course. But despairing? Certainly not, because you know that spiritual highs are part of life, but not all of life. No one, no matter how talented, flits from height to height without ever experiencing a down day, an arid period, or a mediocre moment. In fact, mountaintop experiences are the exception. More common is day-to-day labor on the plain.

Special spiritual moments are God's way of encouraging you and motivating you. With them He offers to you a glimpse of what's ahead in your journey with Him. Like a panoramic view from the top of a mountain, it lets you know that there's a great big world out there, and you are part of it.

Thank You, dear God, for mountaintop experiences! Amen

A Goal in Mind

Have a purpose in life, and having it,
throw into your work such strength of mind
and muscle as God has given you.
Thomas Carlyle

Something as simple as the photo of a son or daughter grinning from ear to ear...a flyer describing the vacation you long to take...a picture of the house you'd like to build someday...any one of these helps to keep your focus on why you're doing what you're doing from day to day.

Yes, today it's tedious and maybe you're even going through a tough patch. Wouldn't it be easier to call it quits? Easier, yes, but at what cost? At the cost of not being able to give a child the chance you didn't have... putting off a dream holiday for yet another year, or even another...staying where you are now for who knows how long.

If daily tasks and responsibilities are getting you down, put the rewards in front of your eyes. A picture, a word, a scene—it doesn't matter. Look at it for a moment each day to remind yourself what makes it all worthwhile for you.

Dear God, I'm grateful for the blessing
of being able to work toward a worthwhile goal. Amen

Celebrate Successes

Always bear in mind that your own resolution to succeed
is more important than any other one thing.
Abraham Lincoln

Perhaps you have no problem celebrating big events like Thanksgiving, Christmas, and Easter...birthdays, graduations, weddings, and anniversaries. But what about smaller, less conspicuous occasions? The successful completion of a home project...the close of a profitable quarter at work...the mastery of a piece of music, finishing point of a special craft, conclusion of a series of tests? Or what about the sigh of relief as you're arriving home after an especially stressful day?

Any one of these deserves a note of recognition. Celebrating small successes spurs you on to further success. As you get more and more accustomed to succeeding at small things, you'll find yourself increasingly motivated to stick with all tasks until they're finished. After all, you remember the last celebration—a bowl of warm popcorn? A cup of hot cocoa?—and you smile. Yes, you'll do it again.

Celebrate the blessings—the big ones, for sure, and the small ones, too!

Dear God, thank You for all the reasons
You have given me to celebrate! Amen

Forever Friends

A friend is a gift you give yourself.
Robert Louis Stevenson

The years bring many changes, including among those we cherish as friends. Some friends we've known for years, even decades, may pursue different interests or a new way of life, and we have less in common with them now than we did earlier. Others may share a certain time and place with us, but then the events of their lives pull them in another direction.

Also, we ourselves change as our lives grow, develop, and broaden to include other goals and opportunities. At each new stage, we meet new people, and with some we'll find a great deal in common. Among them we might even be privileged to find a close, longtime friend.

Hold tightly to the friends you have now, but not so tight that neither of you can grow. Open your arms wide to receive others who enter your life, but not so wide that you cannot embrace that one special person you will call your friend. Despite all that changes, however, one thing remains constant, and that's the forever friendship God desires with you.

Thank You, dear God, for my friends.
Grant that I may cherish the old and welcome the new. Amen

In the Outcome

Let us work as if success depended upon ourselves alone,
but with heartfelt conviction that we are doing nothing,
and God everything.
Ignatius Loyola

Even though we may work extremely hard to reach
a certain goal, we don't always get the outcome we
want. Then we beat up on ourselves, don't we? But it's
possible that our time, talent, dedication, and effort
brought exactly the results that God had in mind.

Goals and objectives help you keep heading in the
same direction as you go about your work from day to
day. But once you've done everything to the best of your
ability to get where you want to go, get out of the way!
Step back and see what God may have been planning
all this time. Perhaps it will match exactly what you
envisioned, and if it does, rejoice that He has chosen to
work through you to such a good end!

But if the results are different, look and see what
God has prepared for you. Let Him show you your present opportunities and how you can use His results to
your benefit and for the wellbeing of others.

In all my doings, dear God, help me see Your hand at work
and use the opportunities you open to me. Amen

Who's in Charge?

I am the Almighty God.
Genesis 17:1

Who's in charge? That's what we want to know when we're looking for definitive answers to our questions, seeking redress for a complaint, or needing guidance to help us solve a problem. To whom can we go?

Many people might go to themselves. They formulate answers based only on their personal knowledge and experience. They remedy problems their own way, doing whatever appears easy and convenient at the moment. Still other people might go to the world—that is, popular judgment, current perceptions, and public opinion. But neither source of authority is dependable, because neither human intelligence nor popular opinion is in charge.

Then who's really in charge? God is. Always has been, always will be. When you need answers, ask Him. When you have a complaint, take it to Him. When you're looking for guidance, go to the one who's not only in charge, but possesses the authority and the willingness and the power to make things happen!

Dear God, I accept no other authority for my life than You.
Let me come to You with all that's on my mind today! Amen

Envision His Vision

The strength of man consists in finding out
the way in which God is going,
and going in that way, too.
Henry Ward Beecher

As you get to know God better, you learn more about His vision for the world around you. You realize, too, that He rarely forces instant change on human events, but instead sends out His servants to produce change in the course of time. That is, He sends out people like you.

God gives you the privilege of making His vision real in the world. You do it with every small, even routine, thoughtful gesture and kindly word. You do it whenever you set a godly example, conduct yourself with honesty and integrity, and treat others the way you want them to treat you. Each time you stand up for what's right, take a compassionate view, and work for understanding and peace, you help make His vision visible among people.

Many would claim that God's vision is an ideal and not workable in the real world. All the while, God's servants are going about making it happen little by little, day by day. Perhaps it's because they simply refuse to settle for less than love, pure love.

Thank You, dear God, for the privilege
of bringing Your vision into reality among people. Amen

A Godly Guide

*The voice of conscience is so delicate
that it is easy to stifle it; but it is also so clear
that it is impossible to mistake it.
Madame de Staël*

"Let your conscience be your guide" is good advice, except when we muzzle our conscience. Each time we choose convenient fixes over the right thing...easy solutions over compassionate answers...hidden gain over open honesty, we muffle the voice of conscience. When conscience dares speak up, we silence it with dubious reasoning and questionable excuses.

Your conscience is a worthy guide when you allow God to shape and mold it with His timeless truths. When you do, you can depend on it to give you good counsel, and you can expect it to shout No! from time to time. Listen to its voice and obey it! Your conscience is there to nix moral short-cuts that would distance you from being the person God wants you to be.

Let the voice of your God-shaped conscience guide you to a good reputation, earned respect, proven integrity, firm self-worth, and—sweetest of all—peaceful, restful nights.

**Dear God, let my conscience speak with Your wisdom
and my actions follow its voice. Amen**

Generosity Starts Now

He that gives all, though but little, gives much,
because God looks not to the quantity of the gift,
but to the quality of the givers.
Francis Quarles

The most generous people aren't necessarily the wealthiest people. Sure, when someone donates millions of dollars to an aid organization or to support a civic cause, their largess makes the news. As a percentage of their wealth, however, their millions sometimes don't match the generosity of people on modest incomes, even people considered poor.

Generosity doesn't increase as wealth increases, but as gratitude increases. Those who are thankful for God's blessings trust God to supply their needs. They have no problem sharing a generous portion of their resources with others; in fact, they do so cheerfully. It's a way of thanking God for the ability and opportunity He has given them to work and earn what they need.

Why wait until you have millions? Generosity starts today with the gift of your time, attention, and practical aid to someone who lacks the many blessings God has given you in your life.

Dear God, fill my heart with gratitude
and my hands with generosity. Amen

God's Definitions

What concerns me is not the way things are,
but rather the way people think things are.
Epictetus

Many words share two definitions: the straightforward one in the dictionary and the emotion-laden one in the human heart. For example, words like age, beauty, success, love—you know what those words mean, but what feelings come to mind when you hear them or think about them? If your emotions are destructive, it's time for some new definitions.

Age is a word that can elicit derisive jokes, scornful stereotypes, and even feelings of dread. But God blesses us with age! Each year of life is rich with opportunities to appreciate His gifts, serve others, and grow in spiritual wisdom. Who wouldn't call that a big plus? Also Beauty and Success. Those words can bring on self-criticism and frantic striving. But defined by God, they point to the God-given goodness in our hearts and the Spirit-driven response to His presence in our lives. Two big plusses!

What about love? Love is something we feel, and our feelings are fleeting. The real, eternal, and unchanging definition of Love is God. An eternal plus!

Dear God, fill my heart and mind with positive
and helpful definitions of the words I hear and use. Amen

Graceful Goodbyes

I make the most of all that comes and the least of all that goes.
Sara Teasdale

As we progress from childhood to adulthood, we outgrow childish thinking and interests. Yet once we reach adulthood, we might still cling to an image of who we were at one point or the ideals we held in an earlier stage of life.

Growth means not only heartily welcoming the new, but saying a graceful goodbye to the old. Who you once were, what you used to value, the dreams you so deeply cherished served you well at one time, but they may not be right for today. If you continue to clutch them, or allow them to keep you captive, you have no room in heart or mind for all the rich blessings God has for you in this present season.

Spiritual growth, too, takes place with a continuing willingness to let go of sentimental feelings about God and grab hold of His vigorous and vibrant promises to you. While a simple concept of His presence led you to discover more about Him, it's time now to let His deeper truths take hold.

Lead me, dear God, to a deeper knowledge of You. Amen

Savor the Day

A great obstacle to happiness
is to expect too much happiness.
Bernard de Fontenelle

We thrive on having doors of opportunity in front of us, but many of us open far too many at one time. Like a kid at the dessert table whose eyes are bigger than his stomach, our multiple opportunities in the areas of work, play, helping, and entertainment number far beyond the hours we have to pursue them.

If dozens of fun, interesting, and voluntary activities leave you exhausted at week's end, why not pare down the list? For now, pick one or two you can take real pleasure in doing and leave the rest until next year, or perhaps the year after that. Sure, it's hard to choose, because they're all things you enjoy doing or believe are important. But as at the dinner table, a few savored morsels bring more delight than many quickly swallowed servings.

Some people take a lot of pride in how many activities they can cram into their calendar. If you're one of them, it might help to remember that even God didn't choose to create the world in a day!

Dear God, help me choose those activities
that are right for me today. Amen

A Laugh a Day

Mix a little foolishness with your serious plans.
It is lovely to be silly at the right moment.
Horace

Humor, spontaneity, fun—do those words ever describe what goes on in your home? Your workplace? Your interest groups?

Perhaps we're hesitant to break the steady rhythm of the day with a lilting interlude. Will people think we've suddenly turned giddy or frivolous? Would one lighthearted moment taint a hard-earned reputation for seriousness and dependability? Will our position of authority as parent, manager, or leader suffer because we dared to crack a smile? No, not when humor happens at the right time and the right place. Humor helps, not hinders, our relationships with people.

A playful pause lifts moods, releases tension, and helps everyone regain perspective. Rather than take away seriousness, it restores sanity when tempers flare and renews harmony when viewpoints and opinions threaten to pull us apart. Perhaps that's because it's awfully hard to keep dwelling on differences when we're all laughing at the same thing!

In any situation, "it's lovely to be silly at the right moment."

Enable me, dear God, to use humor wisely and well
when I'm among others. Amen

A Dream Is a Dream Until...

If one advances confidently in the direction of his dreams,
and endeavors to live the life which he has imagined,
he will meet with a success unexpected in common hours.
Henry David Thoreau

You have a dream, but like the horizon, it's always ahead of you. You've said to yourself, "When what's going on now is settled...when I get my life in order...when the circumstances are just right...then I'll do it." But will it happen?

If your dream is taking shape in a practical plan to make it happen, good for you! You realize that now is not the time, but you're going in the direction you want to go. Like a good engineer, you are setting a good, firm foundation for the future you want to build on.

But if your dream amounts to nothing more than a dream? You'll know, because you're doing nothing now, but waiting until everything is settled...your life is in order...the circumstances are perfect. Those thoughts clue you in to the fact that either you are not really serious, or you're waiting for it to drop down from heaven.

It probably won't. There are things only God can do, but many things God has given you the ability to do...and expects you to do.

Dear God, grant me confidence in the ability You have given me to achieve my hopes and dreams. Amen

Go the Limit

One must not hope to be more than one can be.
Nicolas de Chamfort

Along the highway, speed limit signs tell you how fast you can go. In a backyard, a fence shows you where the boundary line lies. Just as real are the personal limits and boundaries that define what's possible for you, but the markers are less obvious. You don't know how far you can venture, how high you can reach, and how fast you can get there by reading signs or seeing fences. You have to set out...you have to try.

The boundary that God has set between what's possible for you and what's impossible isn't apparent until you run right up to it. And when you reach that place, don't fight God's parameters. Constraints are God's way of showing you that here, at this point, you have everything you need for your personal fulfillment and loving service to others.

You know what the speed limit is, and you know where your backyard ends. But your limits? Challenge yourself to find them, because they're probably much, much further away than you think!

Dear God, I take strength in Your limitless love
as I accept the limits You have set for me. Amen

A Telling Choice

If God had wanted me otherwise,
He would have created me otherwise.
Johann von Goethe

Some people are born into privileged circumstances. Their families can provide a spacious home, healthy meals, and an elite education. Other people, however, are born into less stellar situations. Their parents struggle just to make ends meet, and they are familiar with hardship from an early age. But what matters much more than what parents can or can't give their children is the response of each child.

Whether we possess little or much, these things remain true: Gratitude generates satisfaction...cheerfulness attracts opportunity...generosity creates bonds of love and caring... hard work builds self-esteem...self-control frees us to make the most of whatever God has seen fit to give. Most important of all, faith sets our focus where it belongs: on God, not our possessions or the lack of them.

No matter where we started out in life—with less, more, or something in between—where we go from there depends on our response. That's a choice God has given to each one of us.

Dear God, enable me to say Yes to who I am and where I came from.
Let me go today where you would have me to go. Amen

Drawing the Line

When you have decided what you believe,
what you feel must be done,
have the courage to stand alone and be counted.
Eleanor Roosevelt

There's a difference between stubbornness and commitment. All too often, someone once observed, we describe others in terms of the former, and ourselves in terms of the latter!

A better way to draw the line between stubbornness and commitment is to see what each behavior does and where it leads. Consider this: A person never considers another point of view, but rejects it outright. He says he's committed to the facts. But here's where he ends up: Stubbornly stuck in a rut of narrow thinking, faulty judgment, and self-imposed ignorance.

A committed person, however, listens thoughtfully and respectfully to others' views and advice, and is not afraid to change if found mistaken or misinformed. Yet regardless of what others say, commitment stands up for love, fairness, and compassion. Commitment presses forward with the truth, no matter who's against it. Commitment gives life structure and purpose.

There's a difference between clinging to personal opinion and being committed to the facts. Do you know where, when, and how to separate the two?

Grant me the wisdom, dear God, to reject falsehood
and to hold fast to Your truth. Amen

Today and Tomorrow

*You had better live your best and act your best
and think your best today; for today is the sure preparation for
tomorrow and all the other tomorrows that follow.*
Harriet Martineau

Each day holds value for the next. Days that bring us our successes and celebrations...our joys and pleasures...our times of love and laughter are days that lift our hearts and renew our strength. Those days affirm that life is good, fill us with thanksgiving, and remind us that God shows His love and care in wonderful ways. They inspire us to look toward tomorrow with hope and optimism.

Days of hardship aren't fun, but they're equally as valuable. Each problem confronted and solved today proves that we're able and capable to meet our challenges whenever they may come in the future. Another day of patient persistence puts us another step closer to reaching our objective. The setback experienced now, even at significant cost, teaches us what we need to know for a wiser, better tomorrow.

God blesses you with each day and with all it contains for your good. Not even a moment comes to you without the promise of His continued presence, help, and strength.

**Dear God, let me value this day
and all the ways I am blessed. Amen**

Be Glad

Resolve to be thyself.
Matthew Arnold

How glad are you to be you? If you're like most people, there are things about yourself that you wouldn't trade for the world, but others you're not exactly ecstatic about. And it's those traits, attributes, and characteristics you're unhappy with that really get your attention, right?

Personal shortcomings are part of everyone's life, whether they're apparent to others or unseen—or even if they're real or imaginary. Each of us has a bad habit to overcome, a weak area to strengthen, an unproductive urge or emotion to tame, a difficulty we either conquer or learn to accommodate. Yet along with shortcomings, there are blessings—some flower early on and others build up over time. All make up the distinctive individuals God intends for us to be.

Never doubt that God knew what He was doing when He formed you. He gave you life and breath, heart and soul. You possess God-purposed strengths and weaknesses, gifts and frailties, all designed by Him for your greater good. Be glad—very glad—to be you!

Thank You, dear God, for loving me just as I am!
Help me become all I can be. Amen

He Always Hears

There are moments when, whatever be the attitude
of the body, the soul is on its knees.
Victor Hugo

It has been noted that, as long as there are algebra tests, there will be prayer in schools! We might add that as long as there are conflicts, struggles, challenges, fears, worries, and anxieties, there will be prayer in homes, churches, workplaces, and communities—in short, wherever people are.

While you may set aside a special time and place where you reflect on God's wisdom and speak your words of prayer, praise, and petition, God hears whenever you speak, wherever you are. In your home, an inner plea from you for patience reaches His ears. During the day, a private appeal for tolerance or persistence or kindheartedness pleases Him. At night, a whispered bid for peace of heart and mind calls on His heavenly presence and care throughout the darkest hours.

God is everywhere. There's no place you can go where He will not or cannot graciously hear your call, and no time He's unavailable to you. There's nothing you could be doing that would close His ears to your heartfelt prayer.

Dear God, grant me the blessed confidence of knowing
that you always hear my prayer. Amen

Tackle the Problem

Only one feat is possible: not to have run away.
Dag Hammarskjöld

Problems, like pots of bubbling water, soon boil over. Days and nights of worrying about problems only add another problem—fatigue and a case of chronic anxiety. To deny their existence, make excuses for them, or place blame for them on someone else simply prolongs and inflames the issue.

The only way to stop a pot of water from boiling over is to turn down the heat, and the same thing works with problems. Turn down the heat of anxiety by naming the problem in your mind and talking about it with someone who can help in a real and practical way. No matter who or what caused it or made it happen, the problem affects you and now it's yours to tackle. There's nothing to be ashamed of; the only shame rests in not doing anything about it.

Spend some time today at the refreshing streams of God's love and care. Let His cooling waters wash away fear and anxiety...let His presence remind you that you never need to face your problems alone.

Dear God, grant me courage to face my problems
and wisdom to solve them. Amen

It Makes a Difference

To get the full value of joy,
you must have someone to divide it with.
Mark Twain

Joy and grief are meant to be shared. As we hear warm congratulations from others, our joy increases as their words warm and encourage us. As we receive expressions of sympathy and caring, our grief is made lighter and our hearts more capable of bearing its burden.

You may never know how much your presence, your assurances, your loving touch meant to someone whose loss ached to the core of her being. You may never hear how much your hearty praise built up the confidence of someone entering a whole new chapter in her life. Your willingness to share yourself makes a huge difference to the people around you.

In the same way, let them make a difference in your life by sharing your joys and sorrows with them. Let them know how you feel and the thoughts that are going through your mind. Let God know, too. In all your joys, in all your sorrows, He makes a big, big difference.

Join me, dear God, in all my joys and in all my griefs.
Be with me, I pray, in all the circumstances of my life. Amen

Best of the Past

Kindness is a golden chain
by which society is bound together.
Johann von Goethe

Antique stores are filled with objects—both useful and whimsical, practical and decorative—that once were an ordinary part of people's lives. Many of the things we see, like washboards, butter churns, spinning wheels, and hand plows recall toilsome, labor-intensive tasks. We have it pretty easy today, don't we?

Other artifacts, like lace collars, embroidered tablecloths, decorative trims, intricate carvings, and gold-embossed, richly illustrated family Bibles remind us of what was perhaps a more gracious era than our own—an era marked by ideals of civility and courtesy...of faith, beauty, and order...of strength as well as sweetness.

Some things from the past are well worth keeping. But better than filling your shelves with old-fashioned things is practicing old-fashioned values, such as courtesy and kindness, respect and loyalty, simplicity and fortitude, faith and community. Make beautiful things, both material and spiritual, part of your life. Add the fragrance of graciousness and goodness to your every day. Live the best of the past.

Dear God, I want to honor, cherish, and live the best of what has gone
before and embrace the best of what we have today.
Amen

Explore, Expand, Express

Let us remember that within us
there is a palace of immense magnificence.
Teresa of Avila

Sometimes we get so busy that days slide into years and years into decades before we know it. During that time, our hearts become like an unused room—dusty, unnoticed, rarely visited. Sure, we know we have a spiritual space inside of us. "Yes, I need to go in there and look around," we think to ourselves as we pass its silent portal. "Someday I'll do that."

Why not make today your someday? The day you will sit down, relax, and enter the room of your heart. Today, explore your passions...are you in any way following what draws you? Is a new fascination taking shape in your mind, perhaps? Today, expand your talents by trying something you've been thinking about trying for some time. Why put it off any longer? Who knows, it could open a world of opportunity and enjoyment for you!

Today, express the beauty of all the God-given gifts that He has put into your heart. Refresh your heart—your life—with His love for you. Visit the spiritual space inside of you.

Dear God, come with me as I explore, expand,
and express the beauty of my heart. Amen

A Good Framework

There are principles which govern our life—
they are the principles of Life. If our life is lived
according to these principles all is well,
and harmony reigns in place of vexation and struggle.
Henry Thomas Hamblin

Imagine moving into a beautiful home. Everything about it appeals to your senses...the bright colors on the walls, luxurious textures of the linens, soothing music coming from a state-of-the-art sound system, mouth-watering aromas wafting from the kitchen, a plate of cookies awaiting your pleasure. But late that night a storm blew in. Now your beautiful home lies in a heap around you, because it lacked a strong and sturdy framework.

Similarly, a life built on anything except a firm, secure, and stable framework is bound to collapse. Minor difficulties threaten its security, and major problems are sure to destroy it. All appearances aside, it's what's inside—what's supporting whatever appears on the outside—that really counts.

Build your life on God's spiritual values and His time-honored principles. The foundation of faith and stout beams of trust He shapes in you will hold up under any storm your life may bring. And don't worry—He will decorate your life beautifully—magnificently!—with His gifts of love, joy, gentleness, and peace.

Teach me, dear God, Your true, lasting, and strong principles so that I may build my life on them. Amen

True Confidence

Life is not easy for any of us. But what of that?
We must have perseverance and, above all,
confidence in ourselves.
We must believe that we are gifted for something
and that this thing must be attained.
Marie Curie

There are many things that true confidence is not. True confidence is not haughty superiority over others...a brash cover-up for insecurity...a free pass to follow every whim and impulse. Neither is it something you get from people when they praise you, but lose when they fail to notice you or when they criticize you.

True confidence is this: A realization that God sees you as His cherished son...His beloved daughter. From the very beginning, He has had a purpose in mind for you, and He has blessed you with all the skills, talents, interests, and opportunities you will need to fulfill it. No matter what you think of yourself or what others think of you, He looks on you with eyes of love.

Once you see yourself as God sees you, true confidence follows. How could it not? Now that you know you're deeply loved, there's no reason to feel down on yourself, intimidated by anyone, or afraid to go after your God-given desires. You have everything you need to live fully, purposefully, proudly, and joyfully.

Dear God, plant within my heart true confidence
in myself and in Your love for me. Amen

A Time to Hear

Listening looks easy, but it's not simple.
Every head is a whole world.
Proverb

How can you tell when someone's really listening to you? Perhaps it's eyes focused on you and not on what else is going on in the room. It could be a slight leaning toward you, a look of interest and concentration, the sense of taking in your words. And how about this? The listener isn't talking!

What seems like a no-brainer, however, isn't the norm. Most of us are so eager to speak that we fail to hear others. Sure, we'll catch the gist of what they're saying and might even get most of the facts right, but we'll miss their feelings, their attitude, and their point of view in our eagerness to respond. Without doubt, listening takes kindness, patience, respect, restraint, and a whole lot of genuine love for people!

Did you know that you have someone in your life right now who longs to listen to you? God wants to hear not only your words, but He want to know your thoughts, feelings, and emotions. He's interested in the whole story. He's interested in you.

Dear God, thank You for being there
and for listening when I pray. Amen

A Time to Speak

Kind words produce their own image on men's souls;
and a beautiful image it is.
Blaise Pascal

"If it doesn't need to be said, don't say it." There's an easily quoted adage, but it misses an important point. If you were to bar all needless words from crossing your lips, you'd never inquire about your friend's vacation (do you really need to know?) and you couldn't talk about last night's big game (hey, they won; what else matters?). As for the weather today? Look out the window, silly!

Light conversation sets the foundation to weightier discussions later on. Seemingly needless chitchat draws people together, discovers common interests, and conveys caring and concern. Often it delights and informs, makes us laugh and makes us think. What we say veers in the wrong direction, however, when it disparages others, betrays confidences, fuels dissention, and repeats rumor and gossip. That's what doesn't need to be said!

Let God fill your heart and mind with words that truly need to be said, and said again and again. Words of kindness and compassion...understanding and encouragement...helpfulness and insight...inspiration and blessing...delight and good cheer...peace and love.

Dear God, let my conversations be pleasing to Your ears. Amen

The First Move

Courage is resistance to fear, mastery of fear,
not absence of fear.
Mark Twain

It takes courage to make the first move. Many of us would rather stand in a corner alone than step out and introduce ourselves, initiate a friendship, or open a conversation with someone we don't know very well. Our hesitancy makes for very dull get-togethers, and leads to loneliness and isolation.

God intends for you to live with and among people. Your close relationships reflect the love and care He has for you, and your wider circle of friends blesses your life in countless ways. Even strangers—a friendly smile, a helping hand, a welcoming word—are all part of God's plan for you to enjoy the presence of people. And sometimes He asks you to do this: Make the first move. He prompts you to go ahead. Put on your smile and risk it.

If courage still flags, remember that, long ago, God made the first move toward you. Before you were born, He loved you, and He still does.

Dear God, grant me the courage
to put myself forward for others. Amen

Simply Believe

Be still, and know that I am God.
Psalm 46:10

Even the darkest of nights yields to the first rays of dawn. Just as vibrant summers fade under the cool breath of autumn breezes, so the bare limbs of winter finally give way to the new leaves of spring.

The turning of days and seasons reminds us that difficult times don't last forever. While it's hard to envision an abundant future after so much has been taken away, a greening branch whispers, "Believe." Yes, sometimes we need to wait. We can't hurry what's yet to be or bring tomorrow before its time, but we can know, beyond any doubt, that it will come.

In every trouble, be still. Don't worry and don't despair. Wait for God to bring about everything He wants you to learn, everything He wants you to know, and everything He wants to teach you at this time. There's not one thing happening now that will go to waste in the new season ahead of you. Hear God whisper to you, "Believe. Simply believe."

Dear God, guide me through the dark times of my life.
Help me believe in the light of Your unchanging love. Amen

Rich in What Counts

The wealth of a man is the number of things
which he loves and blesses, which he is loved and blessed by.
Thomas Carlyle

It's natural to feel sorry for someone who is poverty-stricken or homeless. But it takes a startling, eye-opening example before we feel sorry for someone who's wealthy—far, far wealthier than ourselves.

Right now you may be thinking of a telling case that you've heard or read about. The moneyed widow who has no one to care about her as a person...the society couple with hundreds of guests at their glittering party, but not one person they can call a true friend...the affluent part of town where neighbors never speak to one another. It's sad!

It's sad when people aren't rich in what counts, and you know what those things are. Relationships that remain true, come what may...friends you can call on, no matter what the hour. Neighbors who knock on your door because they haven't seen you lately...coworkers who take time to visit you in the hospital...fellow church members who pitch in to help you...God who fills you with the richest of spiritual blessings. Certainly you are rich in what counts.

Thank You, dear God, for Your abundant blessings
and for the many, many ways I am rich. Amen

Appreciation Day

If the only prayer you ever say in your entire life
is "Thank you," that will suffice.
Meister Eckhart

You appreciate others, and you show your appreciation in so many ways—compliments and praise when they achieve their goals, support and encouragement when they're feeling down, practical help when they need it, little gifts on their special days. But how long has it been since you've taken time to appreciate yourself? Never? Then start right now!

Appreciate your many successes and all the times you didn't meet your objective, but gave it your very best effort. Appreciate even the harsh realities that have in such a big way contributed to your knowledge, maturity, experience, and spiritual depth. In short, your wisdom—and never doubt that you, in your own special way, are wise.

Appreciate, too, the opportunities to bless others that have come your way, for you have changed their lives for the better. If not for you, then who would have been there? So give yourself a round of applause and a few words of praise. Give yourself a little gift, too. Why not? It's what you'd do for someone else in an instant!

Dear God, thank You for the privilege of my life,
and grant me many opportunities to let others know
how much I appreciate them. Amen

Rejoice
in the Lord always:
and again I say,
Rejoice.

Philippians 4:4